Backpackers Guide to the Globe

An Intrepid Travel Guide for the Solo Adventurer

Kim Heiter & Natasha Weinstein

*I envision a world filled
with women traveling
alone and meeting each
other on the path.*

– SARK, Succulent Wild Woman

Backpackers' Guide to the Globe:
An Intrepid Travel Guide for the Solo Adventurer

Edited by Kelsey Klockenteger
Interior design by Simon Thompson
Cover design by Kim Heiter, Natasha Weinstein & Simon Thompson
Published 2023 by Weinstein & Heiter, LLC
All rights reserved.

Thank you for purchasing an authorized edition of this book.
Reproduction of this manuscript may not be duplicated or
sold without the expressed permission of the authors.

All photographs and writings are original and recollected from
first-hand experiences, unless otherwise indicated in the author
credits. While the authors have taken all reasonable care in
preparing this book, we make no promise to the accuracy or
completeness of its content and, to the maximum extent
permitted, abnegate all liability arising from its use.

ISBN: 9798989175109

Library of Congress Control Number: 2023917552

Printed in the United States of America.
Published simultaneously in Canada.

For Isla Joyce.

*And Eric –
we couldn't have
written this without
knowing you.*

where we met

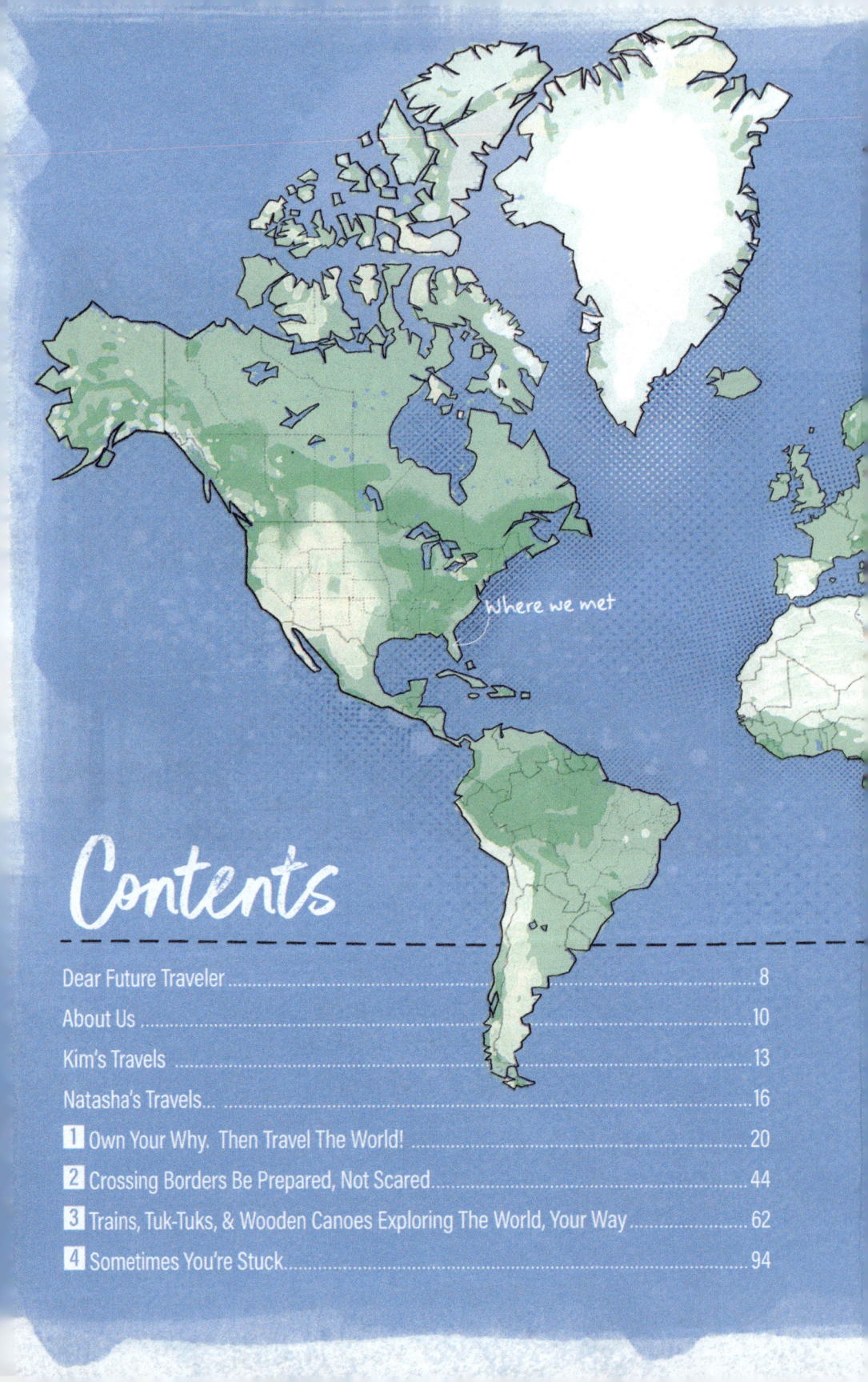

Contents

Dear Future Traveler	8
About Us	10
Kim's Travels	13
Natasha's Travels	16
1 Own Your Why. Then Travel The World!	20
2 Crossing Borders Be Prepared, Not Scared	44
3 Trains, Tuk-Tuks, & Wooden Canoes Exploring The World, Your Way	62
4 Sometimes You're Stuck	94

5 Backpackers, Flashpackers & Bratpackers
Packing & (Cultural) Perceptions 116

6 Where To Rest Your Weary Head Bunk Beds, Couch Surfing, Camping 138

7 Don't Be That Gal 176

8 Flings, Bling & Adventures In Eating 200

9 The Solitude In Dreaming Differently 222

10 Your Evolution 234

Acknowledgements 250

Dear Future Traveler,

So, you think you want to travel. This letter is to inform you that nothing can prepare a parent, aunt, uncle, grandparent, cousin, lover, or friend for your adventures. The truth is, it's hard enough to prepare yourself for what lies ahead, but it is especially hard if you're traveling alone, never mind the considerations you'll face depending on where you choose to go. Sadly, some may never support or understand your desire or decision to travel. That's okay too, we're just preparing you now: not everyone gets it'. Here's a secret we both learned early into traveling (alone) – you'll never truly be alone unless you choose to be, and you'll always be in good company when with fellow travelers.

In deciding not to travel, we limit our exposure to the peace, humanity, beauty, kindness, generosity, education, culture, understanding, and fundamental betterment we stand to gain by simply packing a bag and traveling with purpose to a destination yet unexplored. The information and advice gleaned in this book was often a direct result of our own curiosity, bravery, gumption, mistakes, mishaps, occasional regrets, and sheer will. Most of our adventures stemmed from impulsiveness, stubbornness, or being in the proper mental mindset to spit in the wind and trust it was all going to be okay!

This isn't a substitute for your Lonely Planet, Fodor's, Rick Steves, or any other travel book companion (all amazing resources that we highly recommend), nor is it a simple recollection of journal entries, blog posts, and short stories; further still, this is not written with misconceptions of the realities of today's world, nor with culture, identity, or youth in mind. Through our shared conversations and individual trips and research over the years, we recognized the need for more independent female travel voices, like ours, in the travel category of our local bookstores.

The book you now hold in your hand is our voice realized. Though we have never traveled together, we have independently traveled through sixty-two different countries combined (and counting). Our hope is that in sharing our unique travel experiences, you will feel more confident to travel, even if it's alone. We intentionally shed light on some of the finer, less explained nuances of travel that we, as women, would have benefited from prior to setting out. These range from practical tips on simple preparation and hostel etiquette to the subliminal ethos that guides the international backpacking community. We know the future of travel is ever evolving and often uncertain, but it's resilient too.

The road calls to those who are brave enough to answer. This is both a resource and a calling, based on shared experiences. As travelers, we must preserve the mystery of undiscovered horizons for curious wanderers to explore for themselves, a road that feels less traveled. We hope our stories – written from a deep passion for travel, spirit of adventure, and thirst for knowledge – will leave you confidently inspired to purchase that plane ticket and figure the rest out along the way.

Peace, Love & Coddiwomples,

Kim & Natasha

About us

You know a wild spirit just by looking at them, they carry a vibe that doesn't appear often but when it does my god you won't forget them. They are always passing through lives, never staying put, but always remembered long after they have left. These souls are kindred spirits, they connect deeply or not at all.
—Nikki Rowe, Once a Girl, Now a Woman

Kim

I grew up in a five-dollar home on a million-dollar lot in a swamp. Okay, the million-dollar part isn't true, but it truly was an oasis. Our quarter-acre homesite was a native preserve of true Florida wetlands, hidden inside a mobile home park, a stone's throw from Disney World, and was always intended to be temporary. But, as many things go, it became permanent and ultimately shaped my entire world view before I knew I had one.

My mother moved to Florida from Germany in her twenties and met her all-American hippy prince charming shortly after. Their impressively different cultural backgrounds shaped who I grew into. I had the best of both worlds: structure and freedom to become an independent, free-thinking, stubborn, wild-spirited woman who rarely turns down an opportunity to try something different or go somewhere new.

As a kid, I participated in all forms of activities from classical dance (could never do a split) to competitive roller skating (yes, that was a thing). I burrowed through dirt mounds and climbed trees, water skied and wakeboarded in alligator-infested lakes, skateboarded (to impress a boy), surfed (to impress myself), played tennis and volleyball, spoke conversational German and, when I had time, joined the neighborhood kids riding bikes, swinging on ropes, and picking crawdads out of ditches. As an adult, not much has changed.

My father valued education and saw it as my guaranteed ticket toward a successful future on the real stage of life. I was never expected to be a star student but if I wasn't catching on to a subject, you can bet that my butt was at the kitchen table reading, writing, and saying it until it stuck. He always expected me to go to college, but never actually expected me to use my degree. His philosophy was that college is more about the lessons learned through lived experience than the degree distinction itself. He reminded me this would be the one time in my adult life where I was free and encouraged to learn anything that interested me. I took him at his word. The only caveat was I had to graduate before the money ran out. His forethought in planning and progressive mindset gave me the tools to be successful, even if my version of success didn't line up with conventional expectation. For that and so much more, I'll be forever grateful.

It was during my senior year of college that I was presented an opportunity to travel overseas, independent of my family. What started out innocently—wanting to participate in a two-week study abroad photography course in Ghana, Africa, led by my university professor—turned into backpacking through fourteen countries over the course of three months in Europe by myself!

Two months into my three-month European adventure had found me with a unique opportunity. I'd been traveling with an Australian guy for about six weeks when we were offered an apartment to rent for around US$100 per month in Vernazza, Italy, in the famed Cinque Terre! Clearly, I had no intention of returning home anytime soon. After a series of long-fought phone negotiations with my parents, who at this point were quite panicked that they'd unintentionally driven their only child away to the other side of the pond, did I return to finish out my senior year. The week following college graduation I boarded a plane and set off to spend the next year backpacking around the world alone. I met with old travel friends and forged new friendships along the way, many of whom I continue to stay in touch with today. Every return trip home was matched with plans to leave again. This pattern would continue for the better part of fifteen years.

The open road still calls me, and I find it challenging to sit still. Now married, I pine for solo adventures, not because I don't want to share the experiences — quite the opposite! →

— but rather to prove to myself I continue to be as fearless and capable today as I was then. There's a doubt that creeps in when you haven't traveled alone in a while that you can't do it anymore. The truth is you can. Writing this book has been both a calling and curse because it continues to reignite the passion I have for independent travel while wanting nothing more than for you to experience it firsthand. Be brave. Become irreverent. Travel, even if you must go it alone.

Kim's Travels

1996	The Bahamas
1999	US Road Trip
2002	England, Scotland, Ireland, France, Luxembourg, Germany, Austria, Slovakia, Italy, Sweden, Norway, Denmark, Switzerland, Belgium
2003-2004	Australia, New Zealand, Malaysia, England, Scotland, Ireland, Belgium, Liechtenstein, Switzerland, Germany, Czech Republic, Poland & Hungary
2005	Mongolia, US Road Trip (West Coast)
2007-2008	Switzerland
2009	Italy, US Road Trip (East Coast)
2010	France, Spain (northern Camino de Santiago route), Germany, New Zealand
2012	England, Italy
2013	US Road Trip (East Coast)
2014	Dominican Republic, Colombia
2015	Jamaica
2016	Canada, Iceland
2017	Germany
2020	**The world shut down** – all travel halted (booked and rebooked Japan flights three times)
2022	Spain (Madrid, Soria, & Sherry Triangle)
2023	Remained Stateside – explored Mid-West and West Coast
2024	China, Thailand

Natasha

My journey began as the second youngest of six children. My earliest memories foreshadowing a life of travel were roughly during my early elementary years. My oldest sister had passed down her globe that doubled as a nightlight. As an innately rebellious child, I would stay awake for hours after bedtime staring at the globe. I would spin it around studying the names of all the countries. My fingers would run over the likes of Niger and Bhutan, and I would speculate what fairy tales might exist in lands far away. Curiosity haunted my dreams.

Throughout the rest of my childhood, there were various precursors to my journey. School projects that immersed me in the early politics of Europe, French foreign exchange students visiting for the summer, random road trips with my father (none of my other siblings would agree to go, and even I was hesitant), and then the game changer...the Travel Channel came into my life. I'd spend hours upon hours stuffing popcorn into my face while watching Samantha Brown's firsthand accounts of the wonder that is travel. Unfortunately, my travel musings were not met with complete support from my family.

I grew up in a very, very strict, religious household. Education of the world was encouraged, but with blatant warning to not become obsessed with the creations of man. My pleas to attend a school sponsored trip to Europe were immediately ruled out due to the amount of church days that would be missed and the amount of time that would be spent associating with worldly friends. Anything beyond my microcosm was met with uncertainty and, as a result, my rebellion continued. (It should be noted that I have since developed a wonderful relationship with my parents.)

The transitional period in my life unsurprisingly occurred during the first few years of college (community college, but whatever). A first-year English teacher handed out a research assignment pertaining to the upcoming vote on the "New 7 Wonders of the World." I spent so much time mulling over Neuschwanstein Castle in Germany and other candidates that I ended up failing the assignment and inevitably the class. The following semester I retook the class with a significantly more inspirational professor. Her first assignment was one that has since redirected my life course forever: "Explain a goal you have for the next decade of your life." As I was never a career-driven individual, I announced to the class that my goal would be to fill my entire passport by the time I was twenty-eight years old. It would have been easy to move on to the next year of college with nothing more than a memory of this day, →

15

Natasha's Travels

2005	The Bahamas
2006	US Road Trip (East Coast), Canada, Costa Rica
2008	Jamaica, Puerto Rico, Virgin Islands
2009	Colombia, Thailand, Hong Kong, The Netherlands, Belgium, Luxembourg, Liechtenstein, England, Scotland, Ireland, France
2010	US Road Trip (East to West Coast), New Zealand, moved to Australia (one year)
2011	Thailand, Laos, Cambodia
2012	Spain, Andorra, Germany, Austria, Italy, Greece, Egypt, Nicaragua
2013	Panama, Dominican Republic, United Arab Emirates, Nepal, Indonesia, Vietnam, Singapore, the Philippines, Malaysia, India
2014	Denmark, Turkey, Switzerland, Zimbabwe, Zambia, Ethiopia
2015	Hungary, Czech Republic, Argentina, Uruguay, Chile, Rapa Nui (Easter Island), moved to Hawaii
2016	South Korea, moved to England (two-year study abroad)
2017	South Africa, Canary Islands (Spain)
2018	Guatemala
2019	Poland, Jordan, Mexico
2020	Wales
2021	Greece (outer islands)
2022	Wales, Spain (Mallorca)
2023	Belize, Mexico, Thailand
2024	Sri Lanka
2025	and beyond	We'll see where the road takes me...

but instead I became overwhelmingly obsessed. I was going to see the entire world!

In the following few years, I took a road trip along the Eastern Seaboard of the US and Canada, a cruise to the Caribbean, and a weeklong excursion to Costa Rica, but none of it satisfied the itch. As every year passed, I grew more anxious regarding my incomplete goal. At the age of twenty-one I was on a decent career path, engaged and planning a wedding to a wonderful man, and decorating an adorable home, yet I still found myself enjoying hours of the Travel Channel in lieu of planning my wedding. The obsessive desire to travel loomed over me, and I soon experienced a complete breakdown. I could write entire chapters about the heartbreak that ensued during the following months, but I assure you there are plenty of books (likely next to this one on the shelf) written about that very thing. That's not what this book is about.

The following year, I found myself in a tailspin. On a whim I pushed all my possessions out onto the lawn and, to the concern of my friends and family, I sold (or gave away) nearly every item. A friend suggested impulsively spending some of the money on a flight to Colombia for the following week. Days later we were heavily intoxicated and happily dancing on the streets of Bogotá. We only stayed a week, but the ramifications were profound — I was hooked.

On my first shift back at the Hard Rock Cafe, I'm sure I annoyed everyone I encountered with tales of South America. Regardless, in the most random of encounters, I ran into a longtime friend in the halls, and he invited me to join him at the end of the week on a trip to Thailand. I scoffed at the ridiculousness and walked away. However, the thought loomed over me for the duration of my shift. "Why shouldn't I go to Thailand?" The events set into motion by the following day will forever affect me. I woke up Tuesday morning to find my tax return had appeared in my bank account. I impulsively picked up my phone, dialed my coworker's number, and exclaimed "Let's go to Thailand!!!" By Friday afternoon we were drinking Singha in the streets of Bangkok.

From there everything happened very quickly. I encountered backpacker after backpacker as I made my way through the countryside. I'm talking about the real, dedicated, years-on-the-road-without-a-plan kind. I began acting as an amateur ethnographer and mildly interrogated them on the intricacies of long-term and solo traveling. Within the month I took a terrifying leap of faith and began the fateful journey of adventuring on my own.

DUNEDIN 397 km
VANCOUVER 10,391 km
NEW YORK 12,749 km
CHRISTCHURCH 190 km

(kod'-e-wom-pel) (v.)
to travel purposefully
toward an as-yet
unknown destination
(English slang)

coddiwomple

1

OWN YOUR WHY. THEN TRAVEL THE WORLD!

Never did the world make a queen of a girl who hides in houses and dreams without traveling.
— Roman Payne, The Wanderess

If you decide to travel, get ready because the number one question people will ask is "what's your favorite country or place you've visited?" It comes up every time, and with each new adventure, it gets no easier to answer. Regardless if your travels abroad were positive or riddled with setbacks and sidetracks, each experience adds to the ever-expanding portfolio, personal narrative, and worldview of you.

The following are just a few examples of the highs and lows you too could experience if you make the brave decision to travel around this world. If your most vivid memory was being sick to your stomach and puking on the airport tarmac in the Mongolian Gobi, it's no less your favorite memory than when you stayed up till 4:00 a.m., soaking in a natural hot spring, and watching the Southern Cross constellation come into view between two mountain ranges on the South Island of New Zealand with your newfound hostel mates. Just as for every incredible memory you will make floating in the salt-dense waters of the Dead Sea in the Jordan Rift Valley, you will also experience the struggles of altitude sickness while on a midnight hike up Volcán Barú in the Panamanian Highlands. Peaks and valleys, friends, peaks and valleys. At the end of the day, this entire book is dedicated to presenting you with the daunting task of answering that very question: "What's been your favorite?"

Wherever we're finding you on this planet right now, if we do our job right, this will eventually find you on a plane, train, ferry, tuk-tuk, gondola, donkey, motorcycle, or bus, setting out to explore and therefore writing your own travel story to look back on with confidence and pride.

As we have mentioned, we did not meet until years after we'd each traveled around the world alone. In recounting our experiences, we realized there was information we wish we'd been better prepared with as women traveling alone. Don't take our advice as gospel, rather as gentle guidance with tips and tricks that we (both) wish we'd had more clearly imparted upon us before venturing out. Regardless of your gender, ethnicity, identity, financial situation, or surrounding support system, what we share will give you the strength of heart and courage to set out and join a spirited community of international curiosity quenchers, otherwise known as backpackers.

Maybe more important than deciding where you want to go is when you should go. The simple truth of the matter is you'll never be fully confident that right now is the right time to travel. We're here to convince you that it is.

You'll always have a twinge of doubt wondering:

- Do I have enough money?
- Are these the best (global) circumstances?
- I just graduated and have to pay for x, y, z...
- Shouldn't I get a "'real job'" first? (or) I can't quit my job now!
- Will my family and friends support my decision?
- Is it safe?

It's easy to come up with (valid) reasons not to travel now or possibly ever. Perhaps you're between schools, jobs, or relationships and you know the timing is right, but often that knowledge alone is not enough. Often the single most limiting perspective that stops a would-be traveler from setting out on a life-changing adventure is that no one else they know or trust will join them.

Let's face it, trying new things is scary. Being alone can be scary. Change is scary! So, the question then becomes do you stay home and maintain the comfort and contentment of a life you know or do you step out of your comfort zone and venture forth with purpose to travel your world yet unexplored?

We'll admit, traveling earlier in life (think late teens, twenties, early thirties) is an easier undertaking because you have less stuff. Physically, mentally, financially, and emotionally. For many (though not all) this is the easiest time in your life to throw caution to the wind and venture out. While the stories of those who have quit their jobs or sold all their worldly possessions to finance their trip become less common as we get older, with the right guidance and encouragement you don't have to lament what you did or didn't do when you were younger.

Whether you're a seasoned road warrior or just dreaming and scheming, it comes down to the hierarchy of value you believe traveling can bring to your life (at any age) and having the balls to just say fuck it and go!

Kim

When I was nineteen, I was immersed in the southeastern US hang gliding community where, during a week flying at Lookout Mountain, Georgia, I met a fellow adventurer on his first stop on a trip around the world. I'd never actually met anyone who was pursuing such a feat and was keen to keep up with his travels. We exchanged information, and throughout that year I looked forward to each travel email update and exotic photo that was attached with it. A couple of years later at the age of twenty-one, I set out on my own world travels to backpack alone around western Europe. Sensing my apprehension at adventuring alone, he and his wife graciously invited me to stay in their place just outside London for the first few days to help me get acclimated before setting out alone to explore all that Europe had to offer. When I eventually left them to board the train in the Carlisle Station heading to Edinburgh, Scotland, I promised to call from the hostel upon my arrival to confirm that I'd arrived safe and sound. They said I shook like a leaf with nervous energy getting on that train. I was finally setting out for the independent part of backpacking alone.

When I finally arrived in Edinburgh, I got a bit lost trying to find my hostel. Several road angels took pity on a lost backpacker and guided my way. Eventually I located the hostel, checked in, claimed my bunk and dropped my bag off before going in search of food. In my state of hunger and excitement, I completely forgot to call my friends and let them know I had arrived safely. In my search for food, I learned there's a gap in meal periods where many establishments stop serving food for a few hours between lunch and dinner. I have since learned to always pack a snack. After stopping into several pubs on High Street, where the beer was plentiful but food was scarce, I serendipitously ended up at a backpacker-favorite bar called Belushi's.

Like a magnetic pull, I quickly met other backpackers, falling into easy conversation fueled by many shared tequila shots, but still no food. Among them I met a group of Australian and South African travelers who had been backpacking and bartending around the world for more than a few years to fund their adventures. I was enamored by their tales and envious of their Commonwealth privilege. I learned that many Australians, New Zealanders, and South Africans will intentionally travel for months or years at a time, often staying in Commonwealth countries where their passport status grants them the right to work and earn money, thereby affording them both a uniquely local experience and the funds to continue traveling when they're ready to leave. →

Something changed in me that night, in that bar. The constraints that I'd been operating within my entire life up until that point fell away. I learned of the raw beauty that existed beyond what society dictates. I fell instantly in love with three different people for three different reasons and stayed connected with each of them for more than a year to follow. I wanted to devour life and love and leave this world with no regrets or apologies.

In the end, I never made it back to my hostel that night and totally forgot to call my friends until late the next day—after a note from the kind hostel receptionist the following morning that made clear to me that my friends had called (multiple times) to check in on me. I didn't mean to make them worry and felt tremendous remorse, especially given the kindness and generosity they had extended to me upon arriving in the UK (and for many years that followed). In my very first twenty-four hours traveling alone, I experienced my highest high and most humbling low. I learned of the kindness and human connection that can ignite like kindling when given an opportunity to brightly burn. When you decide to travel (alone), the human connections you'll create along the way are nothing short of cosmic stardust.

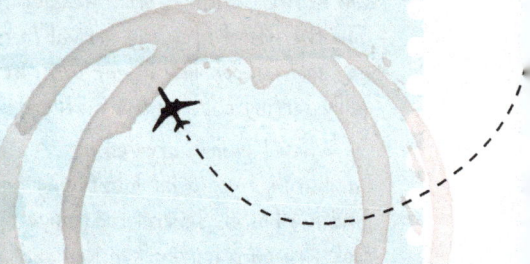

Defining Traveling — Isn't It All the Same?

How is travel defined? Is there really a difference between backpacker, traveler, and tourist? Is there a travel time limit that quantifies your distinction? At the end of the day, does it even matter? In short, no, as long as you're out there doing it with an open and curious mind. All that said, there are minor distinctions delineating vacation, holiday, road trip, backpacking, exploring, and traveling, so we figured we'd try and break these down a bit.

The distinction between backpacking and traveling is slighter than the distinction between those and that of someone taking a holiday or vacation. Whether your worldly possessions are strapped to your back or are being towed behind you is of no concern (except possibly convenience). What matters most is the mindset you leave and arrive back home with in the precious time you have. Americans in particular catch a lot of flak for only traveling for one, maybe two, weeks a year. We are not often culturally credited as long-term travelers, which is possibly where the negative connotation of being a tourist comes into play. →

If you find yourself someplace or with someone remarkable, mark your journal with a beverage ring. Then write a little reminder note of where you were, what you were drinking, or who you were with. It's a cool little time capsule, and who knows, you might even find that same bottle of wine years later and be transported back in time!

In the United States, it's common to say you're going on or taking a vacation, whereas a European might say they're going on holiday—both mean the same thing. In the grand scheme of things, it's a silly distinction, but it's important to note that while we're all speaking the same language, not all forms of travel mean the same thing. We'll do our best to define the nuances based on our own experiences.

Vacation / Holiday

We know life is stressful, whether you're a student, committed to a career, or a parent in need of a break. For these reasons, it's not uncommon that the definition of a vacation or holiday might involve different ways of unwinding for different people. Some people imagine blended beverages, clear Caribbean waters, a theme park, or even full-service spa pampering. For others it's tramping through Acadia National Park or trad climbing El Capitan and then unwinding with a Pale Ale at base camp.

However you choose to get away, a vacation is essentially an outbound detachment from your everyday schedule, possibly involving a passport; most likely including family, a friend, or a partner; and generally limited to a specific hotel, campsite, or cruise line as home base. It's usually limited to one location and often involves a set itinerary. It's a necessary and needed break from your everyday life and can help ease frustrations when longer format traveling or exploring are unavailable to you because of time.

Traveling / Exploring

To travel is to immerse yourself. Immersion includes slowing down and branching out beyond the comforts of what you think you know. What you know matters. What you know has molded and shaped your reality, and that's valid. It's defining and monumental to you! However, what you know is limited and subjective to your defining borders, be they city, state, or country. To step outside these certainties is to broaden the definition of you. Why did you choose to travel to Indonesia, Budapest, Ulaanbaatar, Munich, Bogotá, or Reykjavík? What do you hope to learn from these places in the time you're there? If you don't know, that's okay too. Not knowing is part of the adventure of figuring it out along the way. Be brave and feel secure in not knowing!

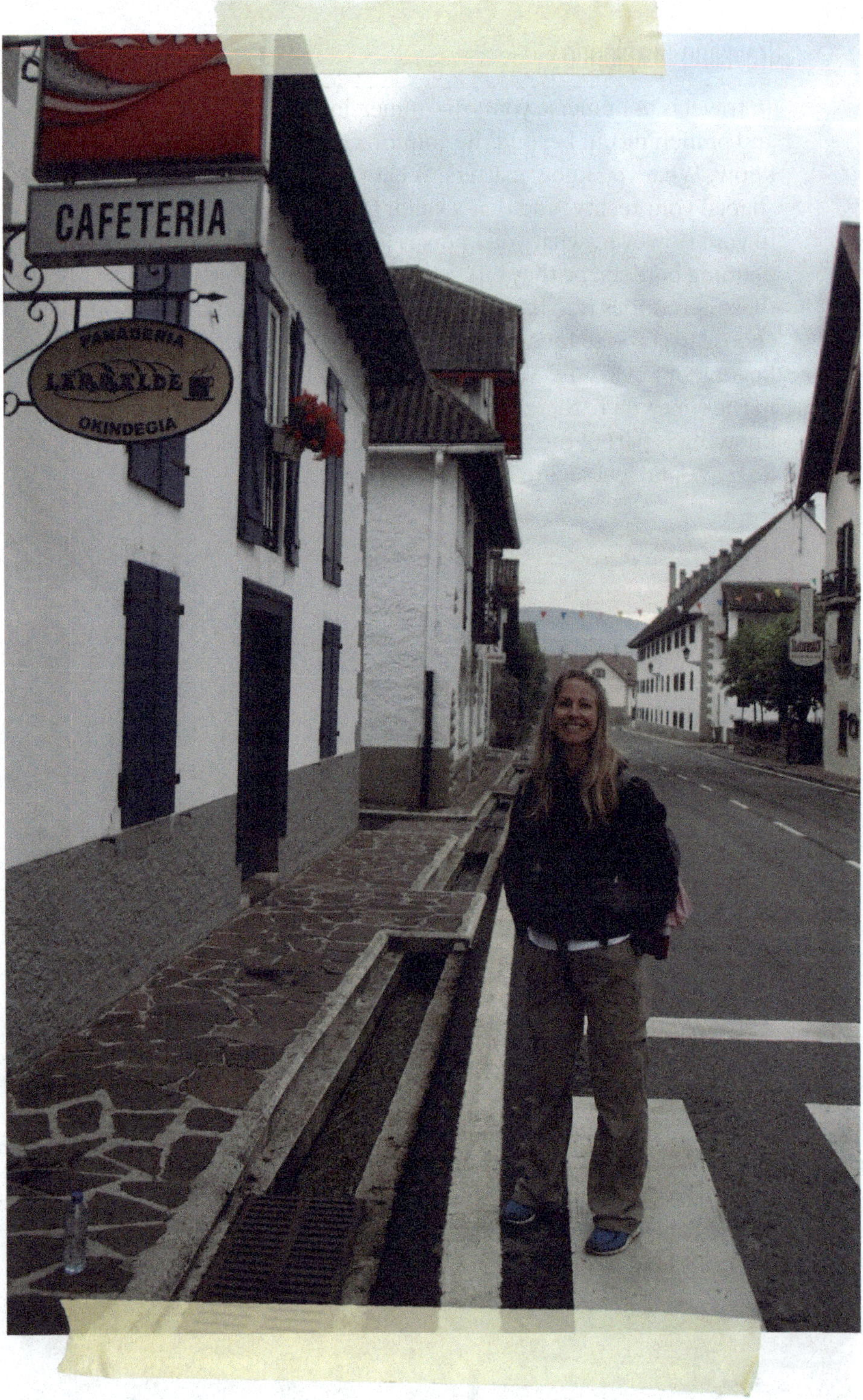
CAFETERIA
PANADERIA
OKINDEGIA

Backpacking

Backpacking requires you to shed the excess of the life you know and survive on the essentials. It's astonishing how little you actually require once you must literally carry the weight of it on your back. In most cases backpackers embark with a fluid knowledge of where exactly they may end up. You may begin with the idea of a specific monument, country, or region you want to experience and simply let the wind take you from there.

Backpacking welcomes preplanning in the form of blogs, vlogs, and guidebooks (including the book you're reading now), but it encourages you to tuck your research out of sight and embrace the unplanned opportunities that no curated itinerary can account for. Shirk the constraints that keep you buttoned-up at home.

Become unexpected! Join that adventure tour into the Scottish Highlands to swim with Nessie or join that group of students heading to Brussels the next day. Intentionally miss your connecting flight and ride a motorbike through the rice fields in Cambodia. The key to backpacking successfully and with the best attitude when things get stressful—because they will—is to try to not over-plan your adventure before it's even begun. Above all else, let go of expectations and what you think you know.

Backpacking can be gritty, confusing, fucking rad, and downright life altering. If you chose to do it, we hope you embrace every moment of it!

How to Live Your Legacy

Now that you've decided you want to travel, the next question becomes where do you go? Think back, where did your childhood daydreams take you? Were you an avid reader, imaging storybook characters fearlessly journeying to foreign lands and wishing you could join their adventures? Did you imagine riding a camel through the desert, the blistering sun warming your face as you peered out beyond the pyramids? Have you ever imagined sipping (boxed) wine under the Eiffel Tower, the sound of an accordion player in the distance, while watching an artist bring a canvas to life? Perhaps your dreams were more romantic, like exploring a tropical jungle by day and listening to the waves crash beside you and a lover while camping at night?

If you can trust us and the process, we can help you bring these adventures to fruition. For right now you just have to have a general idea of where your heart is pulling you. If you're like most people, there's probably at least one place on this planet that you could confidently say is at the top of your bucket list: the Eiffel Tower, the Great Wall of China, the Tower of London, the temples of Thailand, the Mayan ruins of Machu Picchu, hiking through the Andes, or diving the Great Barrier Reef, just to name a few.

There's no rule that says you must go there first or save it for last, but it's good to have a can't-miss destination in mind. Sometimes there are too many places of interest, and you might need to consider a few more questions before deciding. Following are a few questions to help further narrow down your flight search.

You can be just as adventurous jumping on a bus in Florence to tour the Tuscan countryside while enjoying red wine and robust bolognese as you can be trekking through the Abel Tasman National Park in New Zealand, eating a rapid cook provision, and camping under the stars. Later we will go into the distinction between tourist and traveler; this book isn't written to discourage or shame a gentler approach to adventure. Rather, we're trying to encourage less of an all-inclusive approach to travel and more of a figuring it out as you go approach where you experience the byproduct of personal growth and life-long curiosity because of your bravery. It's all about perspective and honoring your personality, who you are right now, and what life finds you seeking from it today. Tomorrow that might change (and if you decide to travel alone, change is one of the few guarantees we can promise), and that's okay.

You do you!

How much time do you have?
- One week?
  (Typical for most Americans)
- One to two months?
  (Great for a mid-career sabbatical)
- Open-ended?
  (Hooray, you just quit your job!)

Do you like a warm, cold, or temperate climate?
- Time of year will also factor in here. For example, summer in Australia is during winter in North America. If you prefer colder climates, head south during the summer break. This is a great hack if you're trying to avoid large crowds of tourists who might also be trying to travel during those busy summer months. Trust us when we say Europe in the summer is slammed!

What do you want to learn, experience, and embrace?
- What cultures fascinate you? This can really help narrow down the list of countries you want to visit. Maybe you enjoy photography and imagine capturing the vivid color bursts of the ancient Hindu festival Holi and posting them on your Instagram. Perhaps you're a foodie and dream of tasting your way through the wild and exotic flavors you'll find in the Khlong Toei Market in Bangkok, Thailand.

Do you speak another language?
- Maybe you want to put those two years of French studies to the test. Perhaps you grew up bilingual and want to visit the country of your heritage. While certainly not a requirement, speaking another language can be a great advantage in helping plan your first solo travel destination. Not only will it give you confidence in getting around, but you'll also become a resource for other travelers you meet and explore with!
- Perhaps you want to challenge yourself with how to explore a country when you don't speak another language outside of your native tongue. Discovering there is a universalness to communication and understanding when traveling around the world is pretty amazing and something to be experienced first-hand.

Are you seeking adventure or relaxation?"
- If you're the type of person who just can't sit still, look into countries that offer a variety of adventures. These can be as tame as guided walking tours, whale watching, and authentic culinary classes to skydiving, swimming with sharks, and naked zorbing!

Money

Probably the next most important consideration outside of when and where to travel is with what money? This is where most people get stuck, discouraged, or just give up altogether believing what they are dreaming of is simply too expensive and therefore impossible. Unfortunately, this is a common hurdle and genuine misconception that, with a little forethought, some planning, and a grand sense of adventure, can be overcome! Ask any traveler and they'll agree: the most expensive consideration of an overseas adventure is the cost of getting there. In part this is because we stick to society's rules of when to travel and don't break them to create our own.

For example, summer in Europe is equal parts amazing, hot, and crowded. Everyone from America and Europe are off for summer break, and the tide of people can feel overwhelming, especially in popular locations. Prices are at their peak because hostels and hotels won't sit empty and do not need to offer deals accordingly. Trains are packed, museums are crowded, and finding last-minute accommodations can prove more difficult. We're not saying don't do it. It will be the time of your life and if traveling alone makes you nervous, peak seasons are the ideal times to meet people. We're also not saying you still can't find deals and travel on the cheap, but it comes at some unexpected costs, namely comfort and sanity!

Alternatively, traveling in the spring or fall offers more temperate weather, lower airfares, deals on accommodations, as well as few to no lines when it comes to major attractions or museums. Discounts abound during the off-season, and it's much easier to capitalize on and really embrace a local culture at a pace that's more in line with their day-to-day outside of intensely crowded tourist seasons. While we dive deeper into each of these topics (and more) within each chapter, probably the most notable expenditures to budget for include flight, transportation, and experiences.

Youth Travel Discounts
Savings for Being Young and Adventurous!

Something worth noting, there are a lot of financial advantages to traveling when you're under twenty-six, a teacher, or still a student with a valid identification card. If you currently fall within any of these categories, check out some of the following discount sites. A bonus is you don't have to be enrolled to study in the country you're seeking to explore, you only need to be a current student.

For around the cost of a beer and a burger, you can travel with a (student/youth) savings card that affords you additional worldwide discounts often unavailable except to those with a valid ISE or ISIC travel card. Discounts include museums, transportation, attractions, hostels, etc. There's even a student/youth specific debit card option that combines your savings right within your transactions!

- **ISIC** (International Student Identification Card)
- **ISE Visa Debit Card** (International Student Exchange Combined Card): Globally recognized and integrated with Google Maps, it offers loads of discounts exclusive to students and youth!
- **ISE Faculty ID Card** (International Student Exchange Faculty Card)
- **IYEC** (International Youth Exchange Card): Great option if you're not a student but twenty-six years or younger.

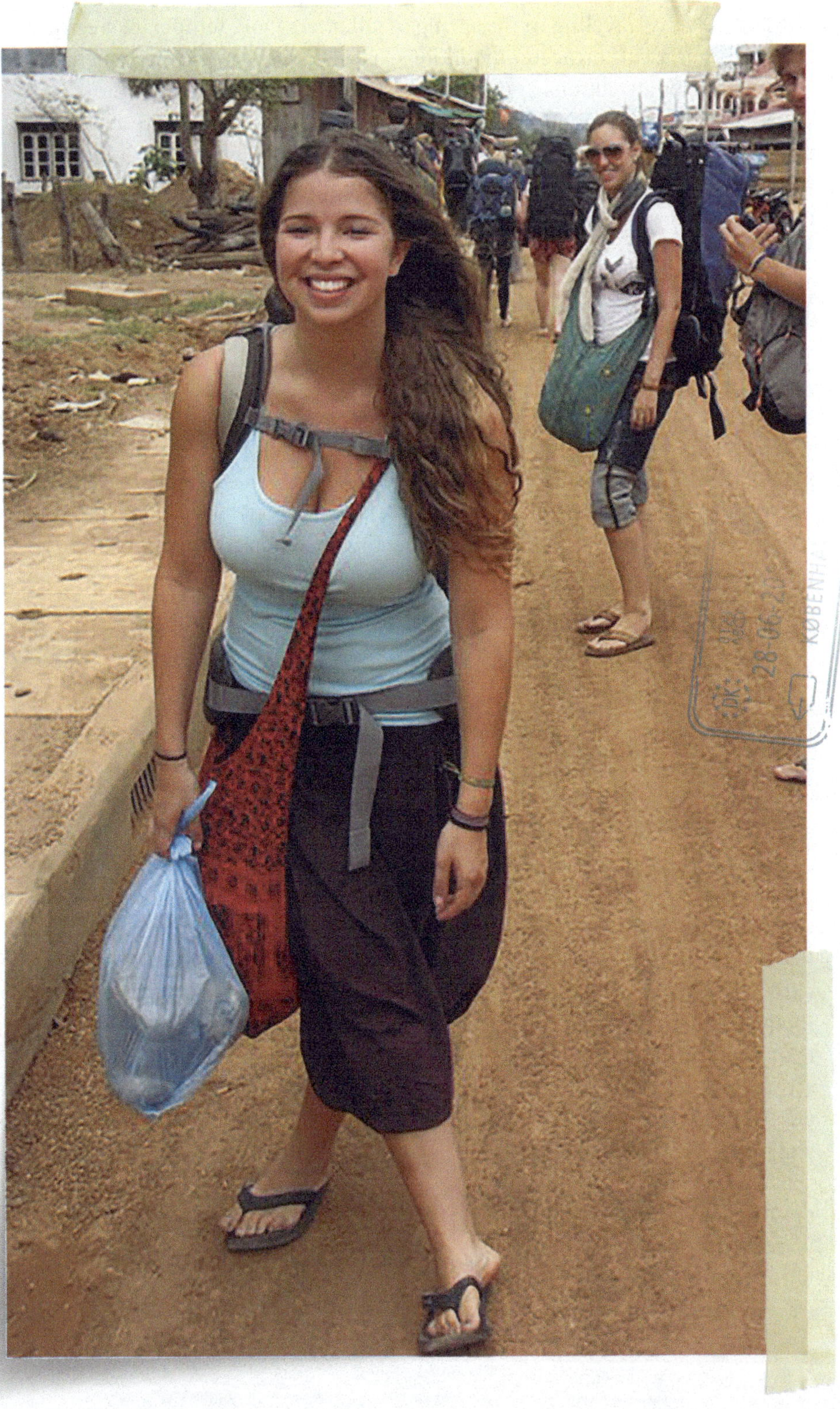

Flights

One way to reduce your dollars-spent-per-day is to front-load your trip expenses. If you know you want to travel and have some time, then the first things you need to budget for are your flight(s) and on-the-ground transportation. These are the single most expensive hurdles that often thwart the would-be traveler. Today there are so many great apps that can help you get your travel savings on track. Other hacks include taking advantage of flash sales. By purchasing that July flight to Peru when the flash sale came up in November, you've eliminated one cost hurdle and can work on saving for the rest.

This is also where traveling in the off-season to a bucket list destination pays off in dividends. Typically speaking, the same flight to Paris in July will cost you threefold what it will go for in March or September. On average, depending on your starting city of origin, the time of year you'd like to travel, and whether you're seeking a single country experience or a multi-destination trip around the world, it would be conservative to estimate US$250 to $2,000 for your flight.

At the time of this writing, a flight from New York (JFK) to Lima, Peru, is around US$435 when traveling in late fall, whereas an Around the World (ATW) ticket via AirTreks starting in Los Angeles and going to London, Paris, Florence, Venice, Athens, Singapore, Sydney, Auckland, and back to LA will run between US$1,699 to $2,269 depending on time of year and if you need to fly into and out of Los Angeles from your hometown.

If you're on a shoestring budget, considering countries in Central America or Southeast Asia will allow your money to stretch further, affording you more options. These destinations may require a little more effort to get to but you'll be more financially flexible than in Europe or Australia in the summer.

Transportation

The next consideration you will want is to try and front-load some of your on-the-ground transportation costs. We break these options down in detail later; however, it's worth giving consideration to how you plan on getting from place to place once you arrive in a foreign country.

Some countries have great rail systems in place and don't benefit from or require a personal vehicle, notably Europe and Asia. If you're exploring South America, Australia, New Zealand, or the US, consider purchasing a backpacker car and blazing your own trail. Keep in mind, manual transmission vehicles are still predominantly driven in countries outside the US, and you may incur additional charges for an automatic transmission. #VanLife. Backpacker-specific guided tours, as an extension of your transportation needs, are another great way to kill two birds with one stone.

Trying to set aside an extra US$300 to $1,000 for upfront transportation considerations will make your on-the-ground expenses literally just dollars per day. With those two expenses resolved, you'll be left budgeting lodging, food, and experiences, which can really run you from free to about US$40 per day, depending how savvy or outgoing you are.

There are tons of blogs, books, and fellow backpackers online and on the road all too willing to share their tips and tricks. Take it all with a grain of salt, adapting what works for you and leaving some suggestions on the table for others to apply. As you travel along this path of enlightenment, you'll figure out your travel style and financial priorities, allowing your money to take you further.

PRO-TIP

For a nominal fee, online services like Going can net you extreme savings on domestic and international flights for when you're feeling impulsive. It's a pretty great feeling when you spontaneously purchase an international flight after a few glasses of wine. This way you know you're at least getting the best deal.

Accommodations

While we explore this topic more broadly in chapter six, it's worth mentioning that a lot of money can be saved on accommodations simply by strategizing the days of the week you're intending to explore, the time of year you're going, and the proximity you're willing to forgo (away from the city center) for a better deal.

For example, if your dream is to visit Paris, France, in July (peak season, therefore more expensive) and you have only a few days to explore, why not familiarize yourself with their intracity metro train system and find a hostel just outside the downtown limits, just one or two metro stops away. It's easy to use and by staying one or two metro stops outside of downtown, you can stretch your daily allowance even further.

PRO-TIP

Can't scrape together the extra cash with your day job but still have a thirst for knowledge and travel? Natasha parlayed using a student loan to fund her trip to Indonesia where she took her classes online!

CONFRONTING
YOUR (UN)COMFORT ZONE

'Life begins at the end of your comfort zone.'
— **Neale Donald Walsch, Conversations with God: An Uncommon Dialogue, Book 1**

High School

A road trip across your home country is similar to attending high school. You are going to have a lot of fun, encounter some roadblocks, and learn some incredible life lessons, but it's all pretty much information that you had a basic handle on prior to leaving home.

Undergrad (College/Uni)

Backpacking across regions such as Europe, Australasia, or Central America is akin to an undergraduate degree or your first four years in a university. You will make amazing friends from all over the world. You will party your ass off and believe that it is an entirely original experience that could in no way be duplicated ever again.

Monuments may be seen, some new language may be learned, and a broader cultural understanding may be gained. The lessons you take away from these experiences will shape the rest of your life and possibly influence future business and relationship decisions. Just like attending university, it's not for everyone and you can still be successful in life if you choose not to attend.

Grad School (Master's Degree)

Backpacking across Southeast Asia or South America would be equivalent to receiving a master's degree. While local knowledge or language skills are invaluable, these regions still require a lot more effort to travel through. Some considerations include greater distances between destinations with less frequent transport routes available. Getting to your next destination may benefit from additional research and might even require immunization shots. These considerations aside, they are definitely worth the additional time and energy spent in planning.

You will make friends from all walks of life that you are simultaneously more different from and yet have more in common with than you knew possible. It is likely some may become permanent fixtures in the future background of your adult life. Your patience will be tested, a newfound cultural understanding acquired, and somehow you will still find time to party your ass off!

Natasha

Once, sitting around a campfire in Chitwan National Forest, Nepal, a fellow traveler asked where everyone was headed next. I eagerly answered India. Immediately, I noticed the eyes of a few travelers around the table shift. Nervously, I asked why there was so much uneasiness.

One traveler replied, "Let's just say all of us here are seasoned travelers. We all have the equivalent of a university or advanced degree in travel, so to speak. Traveling through India could be likened to getting your PhD. It will take time, hard work, and perseverance. You will likely be sick to your stomach and possibly shed some blood, sweat, or tears in the process. That said, you will be proud to have done it. Good luck."

The comment made me so nervous I debated skipping India all together. I postponed the trip by months and opted to venture to Indonesia, Malaysia, the Philippines, and Singapore first. My Indian visa was burning a metaphorical hole in my passport as I anxiously watched the expiration date come closer. In the end, I rallied the courage and braved it, but that traveler was right. There were sweat, tears, and more nausea than I care to admit, and it was totally worth it!

Now whenever I am contemplating the next leg of my journey, I can't help but wonder what educational level of travel am I about to embark upon?

A yurt or ger is a portable, round tent covered and insulated with skins or felt and traditionally used as a dwelling by several distinct nomadic groups in the steppes and mountains of Inner Asia

Doctoral (PhD)

India, China, Mongolia, Russia and other dramatic locations: these are where you earn your PhD! Traveling through these countries (or even gaining visa approval) will be some of the most rewarding yet challenging experiences of your life. They will stun and intimidate you, yet you will make incredible connections and have an absolute blast. There will be days when you just want to throw up your hands, throw back a loperamide and just give up. Believe us when we say the knowledge and experience you'll gain in exploring these regions will garner respect for the rest of your life.

Supersecret Spy School

Finally, Siberia, Africa and Antarctica, frankly speaking, are entirely different beasts—perhaps the equivalent to being recruited by the CIA or as a supersecret spy. Only a select few will ever be given or elect to take the opportunity to explore these regions. The beauty and knowledge gained is unmatched and unavailable elsewhere in the world. It will make you smile, laugh, cry, and question everything you know about the modern world. You will leave the experience a changed person!

In the end, trust that whichever path you travel will be the right road. There is no linear guidebook or designated checklist (although we've provided 101 ideas to consider) that is more correct or supersedes another. Remember, there is no wrong way to travel except with a closed mind.

10
Bucket List Ideas
To check off your list

1. Dodge flying tomatoes at La Tomatina, Spain . . . . ☐
2. Release a lantern during the Loy Krathong Festival, Thailand . . . . ☐
3. Take a Turkish bath in Istanbul, Turkey. . . . . ☐
4. Bathe in Devil's Pool at Victoria Falls, Zimbabwe. . . . . ☐
5. Experience the colors of the Holi Festival, India. . . . . ☐
6. Drink a Festbier at Oktoberfest in Munich, Germany . . . . ☐
7. Throw a bucket of water at the Songkran Festival, Thailand . . . . ☐
8. Hike the Himalayas in Nepal. . . . . ☐
9. Get PADI certified off the Great Barrier Reef, Australia . . . . . . ☐
10. Run with the bulls in San Fermin, Spain. ☐

43

2.
CROSSING BORDERS
BE PREPARED, NOT SCARED

Security is mostly a superstition. It does not exist in nature, nor do the children of men as a whole experience it. Avoiding danger is no safer in the long run than outright exposure. Life is either a daring adventure, or nothing.
—Helen Keller, The Open Door

Kim

I remember saying goodbye to my dad at my gate at the Orlando International Airport. This was shortly after the attacks on 9/11, and the restrictions on being accompanied all the way to your boarding gate were not yet enforced. I had researched my trip for months, read every travel guide, and watched every episode of Samantha Brown, Rick Steves, and Globe Trekker I could lay my eyes on. I had laid out everything I could think I might need, cut it in half, then did it again until I had the perfect backpacker-packed backpack that would make Rick Steves proud. No blow dryer or makeup bag adding weight or complicating my adapter situation. No sir! The day I left for London, I was wearing a gray wool-blend hoodie, lightweight green khaki pants that could zip into shorts, a white T-shirt, a money belt with my rail tickets, traveler's checks, and passport stuffed safely down my pants, and all-terrain trail sneakers that could carry me down city streets, up a mountain, and to all the pubs my liver could handle. I was ready to go...or so I thought.

As I stood in that airport, wondering if I'd be warm enough on the flight while triple-checking I hadn't left my passport in the women's stall, I couldn't help but wonder if I was actually capable of traveling alone. Very soon, wonder turned to anxiety, then anxiety turned to fear. I recall thinking, and quite possibly said out loud, that I'd changed my mind and did not want to go. I was dead serious. Had my dad offered to drive me home right there on the spot, I would have accepted, and it would have been the absolute worst decision of my life.

My dad did not offer to drive me home. He did not offer an alternative or easy way out. He reminded me this was my decision and that I was strong and capable and prepared enough to handle the challenges and adventures that awaited me. Leaving for college paled in comparison to saying see you in three months at that moment. Sure, there is a degree of calculated risk in being a young woman alone in a foreign country, but that risk follows us every day, regardless of the soil we stand on. Keep that in mind when the fear or doubt creeps into your own thoughts. You too are strong, capable, and prepared for all the adventures that await!

Your Passport to the World

We're not going to spend time trying to sell you on the advantages to having a passport; we'll only say if you're reading this book and don't yet have yours, get one! Strictly speaking, a passport is your ticket to the world. For US citizens, we have included a couple helpful links in the back of this book to help you get started.

Protecting Your Passport

Once you have your passport, protect it like your life depends on it! We can't stress this enough! Having a backup copy (digital and hard copy) is important, but you should almost never be separated from your passport while traveling. While it's common practice that some hotels, hostels, border guards, and others will ask to look at or make a copy of your passport upon check-in, this should be done within your view. With few and far between rare exceptions, specifically at certain border crossings, it is not common practice for an accommodation or business to request to keep your passport. Your passport must always remain in your possession. If someone insists they must take your passport out of sight to make a copy, ask to accompany them. We repeat: do not let your passport out of your sight!

Losing Your Passport

If for some reason you misplace or lose your passport, it's not the end of the world, though it is certainly a pain in the ass and may feel like the end of the world. Losing your passport will impact your ability to freely explore in the moment and might have more serious or time-consuming consequences. We recommend having a few backup copies of your passport, important docs, visas, and immunizations for an emergency situation such as this.

The first thing you'll need to do is contact the local authorities (if you've been hurt, robbed, or are in need of help), and then contact your embassy or consulate in the country you're in. They'll likely require you to show up in person and have access to copies of all of your lost documents, identifications, and passport. We refer you to our list of preferred backup documents later in this chapter.

Below are a few additional tips to consider.

* Store a copy digitally that you can access via the cloud or have emailed to you by a trusted friend or family member
* Have a hard copy of your documents in a sealed storage bag stored safely at the bottom of your backpack
* Leave a hard copy of important document scans with a family member or friend back home who can help prove your identity should the situation arise
* Have a few extra passport photos on hand; they come in handy for other reasons, including securing travel visas or ski passes in other countries

FUN FACT

Want to know how much clout your passport carries? Check out the Henley Passport Index online to find out your Global Passport Ranking.

Once you've declared your passport lost or stolen, that information is sent to Interpol to be entered into the international database of Stolen and Lost Travel Documents (SLTD) and unfortunately becomes flagged, so even if you find your passport, it's no longer valid for travel. You will also be required to complete a DS-11 passport application, in person, at your local consulate or embassy. You'll have to pay any application fees and expediting charges if you want to continue traveling as planned. You may also be asked for your continued travel itinerary and any flight details you've already secured.

Bottom line, for the love of all things holy, please

DON'T LOSE YOUR PASSPORT!!!

PRO-TIP

Money or travel belts are great ways to keep your passport safe and secured on your person. These fit flat against your skin and are worn under your clothes. They're soft, low profile, inconspicuous, and you can sleep in them. This is where documents and cards should be kept that you do not need access often. Your purse or day pack can hold your cash and items you can access more easily during the day. Sidenote, if you are in a tropical climate or prone to sweatiness, it would be wise to have a plastic or protective barrier within the travel belt. Otherwise, you may find yourself after a full day's hike with a very soggy and fraying passport.

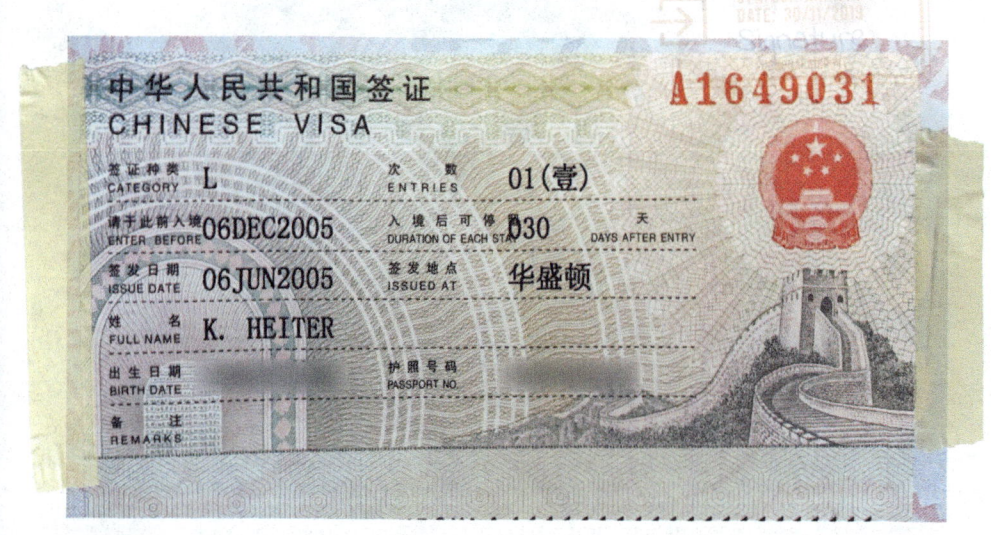

Visas

While many countries do not require a separate visa for entry, outside of your passport, others do. For example, the United States has a travel agreement with Japan and doesn't require a special visa for entry whereas China will require one simply to accommodate a layover or catch a connecting flight.

Visas might be one of the few considerations where we both agree that over preparation on the front end can lead to less stress and more spontaneous adventure on the back end, especially if you're not entirely sure you'll end up going to a specific country but know you'll be in that part of the world. If you have the means and flexibility, why not give yourself the option?

- Visa requirements are unique not only to the country of arrival but to the individual. Seemingly insignificant things like your last name, your passport of origin, or country of birth may impact the steps required or time involved in obtaining approval. It is possible to be refused entry into a country without the proper visas, so do your homework. This process can take upwards of six weeks, so it really is in your best interest to research any additional visa requirements in advance of your trip in the event you need to apply.

For the most part, you'll be applying for a tourist visa. This typically affords you up to three months of travel in a particular country or region. Some visas require specific dates of travel (China for example), so you'll need to know your specific dates and also your airline flight info. Average visa costs range from US$0 to over $100, depending on where you're going. It's generally more cost effective to apply for these directly from the (country specific) government website. Unless you've purchased a guided travel experience and are working with the equivalent of an agent, it's more efficient and cheaper to purchase these yourself. Remember, you pay extra for convenience! Why not save that money for when you're in the countries you're dreaming of visiting?

If you just aren't sure where the wind will blow you, it's worth noting some countries do allow for travel visas to be purchased at their border. Bolivia, Cambodia, and Nepal are just a few where you can arrive and purchase at the border or airport upon arrival. Keep in mind, you'll need to have extra passport photos on hand as well as foreign and US currency. While some countries insist on paying in local currency, many prefer US currency.

If you decide to chance this approach, we recommend having (backup) copies of the following documents since what you'll need to show or prove will vary from country to country.

★ Copy of your passport
★ Extra passport photos (some countries require one)
★ Copy of your birth certificate (in case you lose your passport)
★ Copy of your driver's license
★ Copy of current immunizations, COVID-19 documentation
★ Copy of any medications you are on and/or prescriptions in case of emergency
★ Copy of travel medical insurance (applicable in some countries, post-COVID)
★ Emergency contacts

[Visa on Arrival Receipt — Republic of Indonesia, US 25 Dollars, thirty days stay in Indonesia, stamped 26 OCT 2023, AB 4146856]

Natasha
Personal Experiences Crossing Borders

Cambodia:
Visas are available at the border for US citizens (and many others) for about US$30 to $55 (but expect to wait a few hours during high season).

Nepal:
Visas are available quickly at the border for fifteen days (about US$30), thirty days (about US$50) or ninety days (about US$125).

South Africa:
No visa required upon arrival for US citizens visiting for less than ninety days, but an International Certificate of Vaccination or Prophylaxis (also called ICVP or "yellow card") is required if traveling from specific regions (or if you have a layover in those regions).

Argentina:
No visa was required, but proof of online payment of a reciprocity fee of about US$160 was required before boarding my flight.

India:
While I was in Nepal, I retrieved my Indian visa from the local consulate, which required three hours of waiting my turn, followed by them keeping my passport before it was returned with their visa inputted—a lesson learned. The Indian Consulate kept my passport for longer than I had left on my tourist visa for Nepal. Therefore, I was required to go to the US Embassy to alert them of this fact and then go to the Nepalese authorities to pay a fee and extend my visa. I can tell you the Nepalese government is more gracious than many other countries' if you overstay your visa.

DID YOU KNOW? As of 2024, U.S. Citizens traveling across The Pond will need a 'visa' to visit Europe. The European Travel Information and Authorization System (ETIAS) online form must be completed prior to departure (approval received via email) and will set you back about US$8; at the time of this writing. This new requirement affects about sixty (currently) visa-exempt countries. The authorization is valid for up to three years or until your passport expires. While the ETIAS awards travel authorization, it does not guarantee entry. Be prepared to show your passport and speak with a border guard upon arrival.

Internet forums and travel blogs can provide a reassuringly accurate and up-to-date amount of information answering just about any travel- or country-specific question you may have. It's worth noting that it's easy to fall down a forum rabbit hole. Try to separate the wheat from the chaff and take only relevant information that applies to your query. There's simply no substitution for getting out there and experiencing this planet for yourself. To avoid this situation happening to you, read on for some tips and tricks we picked up along the way.

> **PRO-TIP**
>
> If possible, tuck at least US$100 emergency cash in with your backup documents. You just never know.

Borders & Crossings

Settle in because there is a lot to consider and be aware of with borders and crossings, and the information periodically updates with time and global circumstances. Each and every time you cross a border will be different. These experiences will be as unique as the travelers you meet along the way. It would be utterly impossible to create a one-size-fits-all guide to border crossings, and really that's what your local guidebook will be for. That said, here are a few general guidelines we've found useful throughout our travels:

★ **Be organized!** Have your passport and all required paperwork available to access quickly. On occasion you may be asked to provide proof of funds. A bank statement will usually suffice. Be sure to fill out all customs and immigration forms provided, prior to arrival, in transit or at the border.

★ **Speak respectfully to all border officials.** Do not try to make jokes with immigration guards—just trust us, it's not the time. Remove any and all glasses and sunglasses, hats, or unnecessary head coverings (excluding those worn for religious purposes). Be aware if your photo shows you with different colored hair or a longer or shorter hair style, it might add time to the verification process.

★ **Do not lie** when asked questions about your travel itinerary, but keep in mind most immigration control will not want to hear that you do not have a plan. If you choose to wing your trip, at least have a guideline to answer questions (check out the section below on questions commonly asked at the border).

★ **Be patient.** Try to use the restroom prior to queuing in line. In some countries security is strict, and it could take several hours to cross; copping an attitude and being impatient isn't helpful and won't speed things along. It can be detrimental in these situations.

★ **Do not smuggle or try to cross with any** fruits, vegetables, meats, or perishable goods. On that note, do not—under any circumstance—carry (smuggle) items across a border for someone else. Period!

★ **Never under any circumstances** attempt to cross a border while carrying illegal drugs. Even though some drugs are legal in certain states or countries, it may be illegal to cross with them in your possession.

We cannot stress this last point enough. You may hear stories on the road about a friend of a friend who successfully carried substances across borders using dirty underwear, hidden pockets, or whatever else. Do not attempt this! The severity of penalties may vary, but plenty of countries consider any drug transport punishable by death. Border patrol often utilizes drug-sniffing dogs that walk around inspecting each bag. If at any point your bag was separated from you during transit, be sure to inspect it carefully prior to border crossing. Don't worry about what others might think or the additional time constraints incurred while inspecting your bag. Your safety is far more important than someone else's ignorant judgment.

Natasha

Early in my travel career I was wholly unprepared and often very lucky. My process was simple, I booked a ticket, grabbed my passport, and got on the plane. Easy peasy lemon squeezy. I very wrongly assumed that this was the way it would always be. Buy a ticket, get on plane, show up, rinse, and repeat.

All that was true until I showed up on the UK border with a one-way ticket and a plan to follow my feet. The conversation at customs went as follows...

Border agent: Passport please?
Me: Sure thing—here ya go.
Border agent: Where are you headed?
Me: I'm not sure, I think I will check out London for a bit, then maybe Edinburgh.
Border agent: Hmmm, well, where do you plan to stay?
Me: I'm sure there is a hostel nearby.
Border agent: (increasingly suspicious) Can I see your return ticket?
Me: Ummm, I don't have one.
Border agent: You don't have one? How long do you plan to stay?
Me: (still trying to keep an excited smile on my face) Umm, probably a week or two?
Border agent: A week or two—depending on what?
Me: (now quite nervous) The weather?
Border agent: Where are you headed next? Back home?
Me: Probably France.
Border agent: (annoyed stare)
Me: (anxious smile then BOOM! I'm in the little airport cage awaiting further inspection).

The following hour of my life was spent desperately trying to convince border security that I:

A. Wasn't a threat
B. Wasn't trying to stay in the country forever
C. Had enough money in my bank account to support myself for the duration of my trip
D. Was going to buy a ticket out of the country

After a stern lecture on the importance of properly planning my travel, I was allowed to enter the country.

Crossing Borders & What to Expect

Answer questions concisely and briefly. Don't feel nervous, they're not trying to catch you doing anything wrong. They're simply doing their job and need to make sure you've done yours by taking the necessary steps to legally enter their country. It's not unusual to encounter border checks outside of airports. Depending on your mode of transportation for arriving to a new country, you should anticipate presenting your passport to patrol agents when arriving at an airport, ferry terminal, or train car (this is common when crossing borders in Europe).

Some standard procedures and security questions include but are not limited to:

- ✱ Presenting your passport and/or travel visa
- ✱ Presenting your train, ferry, or airline boarding pass
- ✱ Identifying how long are you visiting
- ✱ Declaring if your visit is for holiday or business purposes
- ✱ Declaring your residence or address upon arrival. This is where filling in the name of a hostel or hotel on your arriving paperwork will be helpful—even if this is only for one night.

- ✱ Declaring if you are carrying any illegal or foreign products including but not limited to produce, meats, or cheeses and if you've recently been around livestock or on a farm. This is important for a lot of countries to help mitigate the spread of disease, not only to humans and livestock, but also to help protect the delicate ecosystems that make many countries so special.

Beyond that, an officer may ask you to look up while they match your passport photo to your face. It's very straightforward thereafter, you'll either move on to collect your luggage if arriving at an airport or continue onward if traveling by train. The more you can do to expedite the process by being prepared, organized, and coherent, the sooner you'll be on to the next stop.

Think like a scout and always be prepared.

Kim

I could have never imagined finding myself traveling with three other backpackers on an overnight train car, making the long journey from Budapest to Prague at twenty-three years old. Sometime after midnight we reached the Slovakian border and were woken up by border guards carrying semiautomatic weapons banging on our cabin door, demanding to see our travel documentation. It's nothing short of disorienting to be woken up in such a manner. Fortunately, before falling asleep, I'd organized my documents, tucked safely under my clothes in my money belt, and was able to quickly hand over the required documentation despite my sleepy stupor and then continue my night ride.

This habit of keeping travel documents safely on my person, even while asleep, has served me well throughout my travels. It's a habit I recommend and encourage you to adopt. Being organized and prepared when crossing countries by overnight trains will be appreciated by both the border guards and your sleepy-ass self.

PRO-TIP

Be aware that when entering certain countries, it is not uncommon to be solicited for an unofficial "'administration fee'"—essentially a small bribe—to process your entry. While there is no legal basis for it, often the path of least resistance is simply to pay the 'fee' and go.

How was your
experience through
security today?
HAPPY OR NOT

Vaccines! —Immunizations & Shots! Shots! Shots!

We recognize broaching this topic can be controversial and are not here to argue the merits, pros, cons, or politics of vaccinations. The choice in being vaccinated is not a luxury afforded by all countries, and it's worth remembering diseases deemed "rare" by the Western world still exist elsewhere. More to the point, there are plenty of countries where you won't be allowed entry if you are unable or unwilling to immunize yourself.

Depending on how on top of your health you are, you may need to be revaccinated for some routine preventative immunizations. Start planning for any vaccinations around six weeks prior to traveling. Your healthcare provider, local clinic, or pharmacy can provide more accurate timelines per your travel itinerary. There are loads of resources that can help you with the specifics, but we'll highlight a few common travel vaccines below. For a more comprehensive list and up to date vaccine information per country, check out the Centers for Disease Control (CDC) Traveler's Health Destination webpage.

Common Travel Immunizations

- **Yellow Fever (injection)**
The immunization for this disease is the most commonly required for entry into eastern Asia, South American, and African countries. The cost of the shot will vary depending on health care plans and location of administration in the United States. An additional consultation fee may apply depending on where you intend to travel, especially if additional vaccines are suggested. There may be required periods of waiting between vaccines. You should be immunized no less than ten days prior to traveling, though your doctor or pharmacist can provide more accurate answers where this is concerned.

- **Typhoid (injection or oral tablets available)** It's possible to contract typhoid through contaminated food or water in some countries. The CDC recommends this vaccine for most travelers, especially if you are staying with friends or relatives, visiting smaller cities or rural areas, or if you are an adventurous eater. The vaccine lasts two years when injected or five years when taken as an oral vaccine.

- **Hepatitis A (injection)**
A preventable disease, hepatitis A is a viral infection of the liver, often attributed to contaminated water, food, or unprotected sex. It's highly contagious and can be spread even without symptoms; however, unlike other viral diseases it won't cause long-term liver damage or become chronic. This vaccine is administered between two shots, six months apart for long-term protection.

- **Malaria (injection or oral tablets available)** There is no vaccine or cure for malaria, but there are preventative medications available. These treatments vary significantly in administration, cost, and side effects, so be sure to study the options carefully.

- **COVID-19 (injection)**
At the time of this writing, the spread of COVID-19 continues to evolve with regulations and requirements updating in real time. Because of this, confirm travel requirements at your target destination before leaving home.

For US travelers, the CDC does not recommend getting travel vaccines in another country because most vaccines need to be administered ahead of time to give you full protection against a disease. Vaccines available in some other countries may be different from the ones used in the United States and may be less effective. If you're concerned about the cost of travel vaccines and medicines, check to see if your city or county health department has a travel medicine clinic. It may cost less to visit a doctor there than to go to a private doctor.

Of course, it's your life and the final decision on what to put into your body is your own. However, please keep everything we've mentioned in mind when considering visiting certain countries because, yes, they do check! For more information check out the CDC or WHO websites or speak with a healthcare professional about your options.

The name "Colombia" is derived from the last name of the Italian navigator Christopher Columbus. It was conceived as a reference to all of the New World. The name was later adopted by the Republic of Colombia of 1819, formed from the territories of the old Viceroyalty of New Granada (modern-day Colombia, Panama, Venezuela, Ecuador, and northwest Brazil)

10 Bucket List Ideas

To check off your list

11. Walk the Camino de Santiago ☐
12. Abseil the Murren Via Ferrata, Switzerland ☐
13. Experience a traditional pōwhiri in New Zealand ☐
14. Explore the tundra riding the Trans-Siberian Express ☐
15. Traverse the Great Wall of China ☐
16. Mend fences in Patagonia's national parks ☐
17. Gape at the Moai of Rapa Nui ☐
18. Eat gelato in Vernazza, Italy ☐
19. Prop up the Leaning Tower of Pisa in Italy ☐
20. Explore the Castillo San Felipe de Barajas in Cartagena, Colombia ☐

3

TRAINS, TUK-TUKS, & WOODEN CANOES

EXPLORING THE WORLD, YOUR WAY!

Maybe true travel is not the transportation of the body, but a change of perception, renewing the mind.
—Ben Okri, The Age of Magic

With so many vehicles with which to explore, how do you choose your best option? Some points to consider:

Time:

- How long you spend in any one place can influence the style in which you commute. Traveling through densely packed Europe may be easier by train than car. By contrast, you may weigh the value of purchasing your own vehicle in Australia, affording you the combined benefit of built-in accommodations (sleeping in your vehicle) and the option to sell it to the next traveler when you're ready to move on. This can often result in netting back your original investment, thereby affording you more time on the road.

Budget:

- If you're trying to see a lot in a little bit of time (let's say you were only approved for one week of vacation), it's worth weighing the best transportation options available where you're going. If you are short on time but want to explore a smaller footprint in more depth, then you may not need to consider transportation as a large portion of your budget. While it might prove slow, you'll discover more hidden gems by wandering on foot to no destination in particular.

Structure:

- How much structure do you want? Do you live for your alarm clock and love being told to be somewhere on time? If so, then consider a tour! 'There are all kinds to choose from depending on your personal interests. For those dedicating their time to one specific city or region, an informational city bus tour might be sufficient enough, affording you the opportunity to jump off and on around town at your leisure. Multicity and day tours will require a more structured timeline and often include a detailed itinerary of things to see and places to be at specific times. While this approach to traveling will work for some personalities, not all prefer such structure. Until you know for sure (and this can vary by city, country, or region), we highly suggest giving them each a try to see what resonates with you!

Bottom line, figuring out what works best for you is all part of the adventure! We will spend most of this chapter detailing various transportation options that may ultimately influence where you decide to travel. We'll begin with one of the most obvious first-time backpacker travel choices: trains.

Trains

Trains are glorious, industrious beasts that are fast, reliable, mostly on-time, convenient, affordable, and comfortable. They offer the ability to sit back, zone-out, and enjoy scenery otherwise inaccessible by car. We'll use Europe's Eurail for the purposes of explaining the myriad of rail options available. If you're planning to begin your independent travel odyssey in Europe, regardless of where you begin, look no further than the efficiently interconnected rail systems already in place. From local commuter trains to high-speed InterCity Express (ICE) trains traveling upwards of 300 kilometers per hour (approximately 186 mph), the options are limitless for your time and budget.

Trust us when we say there's a pass and approach to purchasing it that's right for you, whether it is buying an individual ticket at the time of departure to pre-purchasing (sometimes before actually leaving home) a more flexible, multiday or monthly rail pass. While some approaches yield more flexibility or ease in planning, there's no wrong way to get from point A to B. Remember, it's about enjoying the journey as much as anticipating your final destination.

Flex passes offer country-specific or unlimited regional exploration in a specific range of time. These are great, especially when you're feeling spontaneous, since you often don't need to stop at a ticket window prior to boarding. It's an amazing feeling of freedom to simply look at a leaderboard, pick your destination, find the best time, and hop aboard. This is an exciting way to end up somewhere unplanned and unexpected!

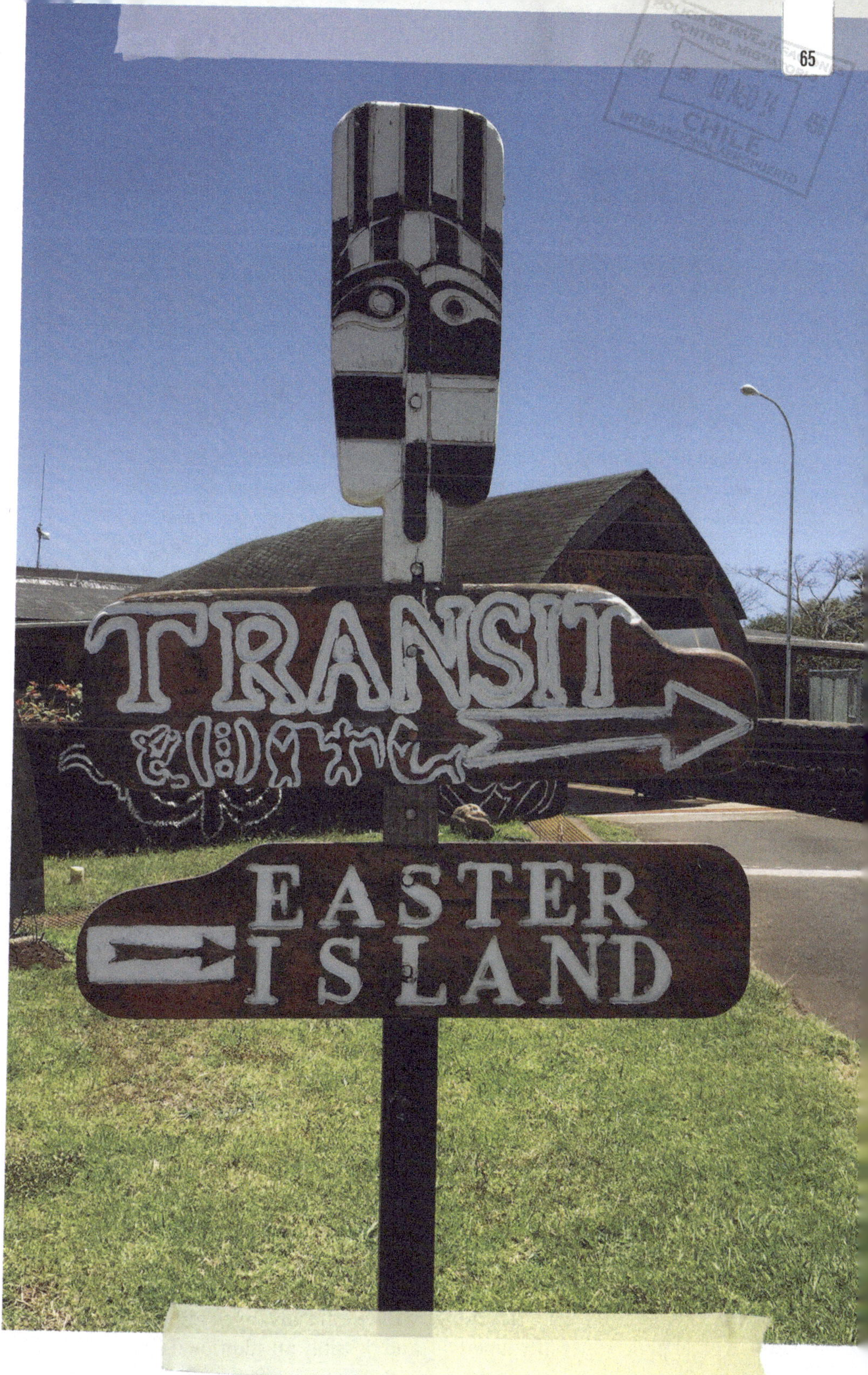
TRANSIT
EASTER
ISLAND
CHILE

With multiday rail passes, be sure to read the fine print and know:

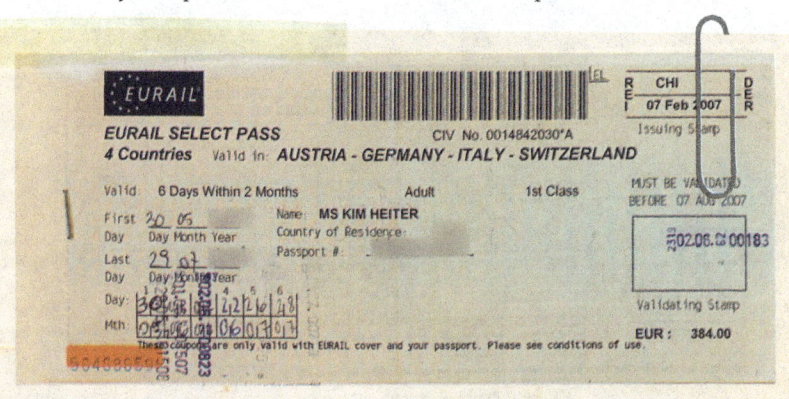

- When to validate your rail pass. Some flexible tickets allow for validation from the conductor when you're already onboard the train while others will require you to self-stamp or write in your travel information (date/destination) prior to finding your seat. Be sure to confirm this before boarding a midnight train.
- What are your travel allowances? Do you have five consecutive train travel days or five travel dates total within a year's time to use your pass? This is an important distinction.
- When your rail pass expires. It can be an expensive faux pas to discover your pass expired yesterday when you're onboard today.

While most Eurail passes won't require advance seat selection, some train lines are so popular that, even if you have a flexible rail pass, you'll still be required to go to a kiosk prior to boarding and get a separate physical ticket due to limited seat availability. This is typically at no additional cost, except time. Plan accordingly.

Speaking of seat availability, it's worth checking to see if your rail pass has a specific train car class notation (i.e. first class (1), second class (2)). If you purchased your rail pass online prior to leaving your home country, it's likely to automatically be a first-class ticket. This is a great perk, especially when trains are crowded and there isn't any coach seating available, however this is specific to you and unfortunately can separate you from fellow travel companions you have met along the way. Often you can claim an available seat in coach to stay with your new mates, but they would have to upgrade to join you in a less crowded car in first class. Something else to consider is sleeper cars. For long distances, overnight trains are a great option to arrive fresh, rested, and ready to explore your new destination. It's basically a twofer: transportation and accommodation all in one! These will require advanced reservation and possibly an additional fee.

Unfortunately, there's no single system that applies to all trains and countries. It's worth familiarizing yourself with your train ticket and saving yourself unnecessary pleading with the conductor that can sometimes result in an on-the-spot ticket purchase. This can really suck if you didn't budget for it. That said, it happens to the best of us but is avoidable.

Kim

Still high on my bucket list of rail discoveries is the 8,961 kilometer-long Trans-Mongolian Express from Moscow to Beijing.

Traveling by train outside of Europe requires a little extra effort and research. While parts of Oceania, Asia, and North America have systems in place, train travel in areas such as Africa, Central, and South America are more scattered and few between. Wherever you choose to travel, be aware of timing connections too closely. While nine times out of ten your train will depart and arrive on time, it is possible for trains to be late, especially when crossing borders, which require passport and ticket checks. If the unexpected delay happens, you could miss your flight or train connection, thus throwing off your well-manicured travel itinerary. We've both been there and done that, and it stinks.

Lastly, take your time in researching the best rail method for your time away. Be sure to check if you qualify for any travel discounts or deals. There are countless resources and rail operators to consider. If you're new to traveling, remember the motto of the seasoned traveler that all great adventures begin when your best laid plans fail. We encourage you to go with the flow and enjoy the ride!

Planes

Flying is a great option for covering lots of ground and capitalizing on your available time in larger regions such as Australia, the United States, Southeast Asia, and South America. Only have a week in New Zealand? No worries! After marveling at the pancake rocks on the North Island beaches, hop on a Jetstar flight out of Auckland and buzz on down to Queenstown for some mid-season South Island snowboarding for around NZ$133 round trip (at the time of this writing).

PRO-TIP

It's worth trying to search for flights from the airline's country of origin webpage and not from your home country since sometimes the deals can vary. For example, if a site asks if you'll allow it to use your location and you say no, it won't pigeonhole your options based on where you're currently searching from. This sometimes nets a cheaper deal. (Natasha saved $500 using a local Chilean site for her flight to Easter Island—she just needed help purchasing the flight in Spanish).

Below are some of our favorite tried and true budget airlines, but you can also find sweet deals directly from major carrier sites, especially if your dates are flexible. Deals can start as low as US$20. It's even possible to find deals for the cost of taxes and fees. Seriously!

- Jetstar • Ryanair • Aer Lingus
- Virgin Australia • AirAsia
- LOT • easyJet • Norwegian
- LATAM • PLAY • COPA

Cars, Vans, and Personal Vehicles

Options vary from renting, purchasing, ride sharing, taxiing, to good old fashion hitchhiking. If you opt to hitchhike, trust your gut and use good ole fashioned common sense! Cars are ideal for short trips, close borders, or exploring at a leisurely pace. We both agree having a car when exploring certain countries will be a great advantage to you, especially when wanting to access more remote locations. As mentioned previously, be prepared that your vehicle may (likely) be a manual transmission—stick shift. Honestly, once you get comfortable transitioning in and out of first gear (be prepared to stall a few times if you're just learning) the rest is cake.

In certain countries there is an understood rite of passage in purchasing and reselling backpacker vehicles. For example, if you decide to travel through New Zealand for a month (or more) and are flying into Auckland, it might be worth asking around at your hostel if anyone is selling their car. While you could certainly look online and, in some cases, purchase prior to arriving in the country, there's a certain rite of passage in handing off the keys in person. Sometimes you can even score extra gear for cheap or free, such as camping gear, cooking equipment, and other gently used items. This is a great way to save on accommodations as certain countries are extremely camping friendly!

> **PRO-TIP**
> Just because a word looks like gasoline doesn't mean it is. Triple check what type of fuel your vehicle takes and that what you're filling with is indeed gasoline (petrol) and not diesel (gazole).

To summarize the lifecycle of a backpacker vehicle, a traveler will purchase a car or van, drive it around for the duration of their trip, then sell it to the next backpacker in need, the relationship being symbiotic. The aforementioned backpacker receives a vehicle and sense of freedom, while the previous traveler recoups a portion of their travel funds, thereby further financing their explorations. ➜

Another personal vehicle option is a rental car. While not always the most cost effective, it's a viable option to be considered. Should you decide to rent a car, be sure to read the fine print of your contract for both hidden fees and country specific restrictions (such as minimum driver's age). Most rental companies will require you to put down a credit card and place a financial hold on it for incidentals. This could range from US$100 to $1,000. While most operations are reputable, it's not uncommon in some countries to encounter challenges or outright refusals to have that hold removed upon returning your vehicle.

Kim

This simple piece of advice saved me from forfeiting US$1,000 when I returned my rental car in Jamaica. I had been teaching in a rural community and needed a rental car to make the thirty-minute commute each day. The claim was that I had put scratches on the vehicle that supposedly came from tree limbs brushing the car while driving on overgrown rural roads. They did not want to release the US$1,000 incidentals hold they had placed on my credit card. Having both video and photo documentation of the vehicle from the first day I picked it up was the only thing that changed the tide of that conversation. It's not uncommon to be strong-armed by a man, especially as a woman in a foreign country—having concrete documentation removed the he said, I said and made my claim emphatically true. They released the hold (begrudgingly) and I went on my merry way.

PRO-TIP

Before you drive off any car rental lot, document the entire vehicle! Take close-up and far away photos of the car, being sure to note and capture any existing dings, scratches, or dents. Then take a slow 360-degree video of the entire vehicle. Do not allow any rental agent to pressure you to speed up or hinder your documentation process.

Something else to keep in mind is that some cars are set up with the driver's side on the left (US) while others are on the right (UK, Jamaica, and many others). This will also impact what side of the road you're driving on. When you're first starting out driving in a foreign country whose road rules and signs vary from your home country, take your time to acclimate. The learning curve really isn't that steep, and it can be quite fun. Just be mindful to take your time, there's no sense in being in a hurry, and feel confident that your driving skills have prepared you for this fun new challenge.

PRO-TIP

When exiting an airport, look for taxi drivers who are respectfully keeping their distance, often a short walk from the exit doors and chaos of arrivals and departures. These are often individuals who won't try and rip you off or aren't affiliated with a local hotel that capitalizes on unsuspecting travelers. Upon arriving in a new country, leaving the airport is often the most stressful and vulnerable moment of the trip. We encourage you to check with airport attendants upon arrival to find the safest options for securing a ride.

Rideshares & Taxis

It is unlikely that you will make it through an entire trip without experiencing at least one rideshare or taxi ride, especially in large cities. This form of transportation can quickly eat into your budget and is only suggested for short-distance travel. If you're in a cab, it is in your favor to insist on the use of the internal meter. If the driver refuses or one is not present, always agree upon a set price prior to entering the vehicle.

- Confirm the make of the car and driver's name prior to entering the vehicle. At train stations and airports, wait in designated pick-up locations.
- Confirm they accept your method of payment. Obtain local currency (usually an option at larger airports) before entering the vehicle if necessary.
- If you don't speak the language where you're arriving, ask an attendant in the station to guide you to the correct place to wait.
- In some cases, drivers will attempt to sell you on a hotel that offers them a commission upon your arrival. Any negative claims that they make regarding your accommodation should be taken with a grain of salt until you see it for yourself.

When utilizing rideshares, applying the same safe practices you would at home is recommended.

We'll talk more about accommodations later, but by no means do these need to be booked in advance of your arrival (unless there's a crazy festival or something, then it's advised).

Traveling alone can be intimidating and will push you out of your comfort zone, but people genuinely will want to help you get where you need to go. All you have to do is ask!

A NOTE ON HITCHHIKING

While this is still a very reliable and widely practiced form of travel, please take into account your environment, cultural norms, and the gut instincts that will ultimately guide and keep you safe. It is always wise to speak with your host or hostel workers about hitchhiking in the area; more often than not they can help you determine if it is common and deemed safe in the region. As women we have both hitchhiked in various countries with no issue; however, these were not decisions either of us entered into lightly or without informing friends, family, or fellow travelers when we were leaving, where we intended to travel, and when we expected to arrive. Use your discretion. Traveling is all about honing your instincts.

Backpacker Busses

These are great for either longer exploration or brief stints. While the options are wide, ranging from large charter buses to more intimate ten-seat commuters, many countries offer a similar concept, typically led by a staff of young, backpacker friendly, proud men and women from their country of origin. A few examples include:

- TruTravels in Thailand, Cambodia, Nepal, and Bali
- The Dragon Trip in China and Japan
- The Green Toad Bus, hop-on, hop-off in Brazil
- Kiwi Experience in New Zealand
- MacBackpacker in Scotland

These will require a little more digging to suss out which tour matches your personality and needs. Throughout Europe, for example, multiple tour operators cater to young independent travelers. Kim was able to swim in Loch Ness, sip scotch in Oban, and storm coastal castles on her imaginary steed, Monty Python style, by utilizing a hop-on, hop-off (HOHO) ticket through a local tour operator out of Edinburgh, Scotland.

HOHO and Sightseeing City Busses: Each major city offers their own version that range in price from pocket change to quite pricey depending on which additional add-ons interest you. If time is of the essence, these may be worth exploring. You get loads of information, and while you may not make lifelong friendships, you might just be able to enjoy the sites in the company of like-minded strangers and grab a beer afterwards.

You can find a comprehensive list of options at any hostel or city welcome center for backpacker specific tours. There's usually a display of business flyers, advertising can't-miss city highlights and tours, sometimes with a coupon attached. You can also see if your hostel offers a specific discount with any operation. This is another great way to save money! If you're trying to plan some adventures before leaving your hometown or country, →

PRO-TIP

Just arrived somewhere new but don't want to commit to an accommodation just yet? Simply ask you driver to drop you off in the city center, then find a cafe, grab a coffee, and ask for a few recommendations. If you're arriving at night, we advise just booking your first night and then in the morning, when a bit more rested, you can explore the area to find your best option. You'll be that much more a traveler than a tourist for doing so.

we recommend comparing and checking online as new options or referrals are always being made available.

Multi-desitination tour pricing (which can also include hop-on, hop-off features) is often inclusive of lodging as well as transportation in addition to providing access to passionate local guides and, quite often, whiskey! Meals are typically enjoyed at local pubs and most evenings end with cold pints and shared travel stories. You don't have to look hard to find amazing tour operators in just about every country on this planet. Consider your options in a real life *Choose Your Own Adventure*.

Traveling by bus, be it public, adventure focused, or informational, may not sound very exotic, however, we believe no matter where you are, you can find an option to fit your schedule, budget, and travel style. If you're like us, then freedom and flexibility are essential when deciding how to get around. Some travelers are more confident knowing certain decisions have been made for them and are relieved there is one less agenda to plan or account for. Both approaches are excellent in their own right.

Let's dive deeper and distinguish that not all bus options are created equal and should not immediately be excluded. While we both approach travel with the notion that the best laid plans are those yet unplanned and that less is more, it's wise not to rule out the obvious and not so obvious advantages of including a guided tour or two as you amble along your journey. For the solo traveler, a guided tour early on in your trip is a fantastic way to acclimate to life on the road, meet kindred solo spirits, hitch a ride, learn some history, and party like a local.

Nearly every city offers a variety of options depending on your spirit of adventure. Want a cheap ride around town with a sprinkle of history in the mix? Jump on and off a guided city bus tour to get the lay of your new land. Love beer, wine, or whiskey? There's a tour for that! Do you have a transportation budget and need to maximize your limited time in a specific country? Check to see if a multicity tour bus is an option. This is great for seeing whole countries like Ireland, Scotland, New Zealand, or the coastline of Australia!

Do your research and talk to those working in your hostel or the random travelers in your bunks—yet another advantage of staying in hostels over hotels (more on that later). There are endless options out there to meet all time and financial budgets.

Intercity & Regional Busses

Bussing can provide a varied array of options ranging from an American Greyhound intent on its final destination to a more languid approach, like in Ireland where drivers are known to indulge their inner tour guide and offer up regional information, even stopping for passengers (both foreign and local) to take pictures of a lovely landscape, sunset, or stream just because it's beautiful. These same intercity and regional bus lines are also known to take the occasional detour to deliver medication and packages to the elderly and remote residents that might otherwise have had to wait or been forced to commute.

Bus options in low-income countries can be as varied as the countries themselves. The loud music and flashing lights of the Diablos Rojos (Red Devils) buses feel intimidating your first time in Panama but electing this mode of transportation will preserve your travel funds with an average cost of US$0.25 per journey. The comparatively calmer buses in Nepal may still raise some eyebrows. Much like the undergrounds of London or Tokyo, Nepalese bus operators will cram as many people into a bus as possible. If you are on a popular route, mentally prepare yourself to share your seat, sit on a friend's lap or cuddle up to a goat for roughly 25 rupees (US$0.20). You may be willing and able to fork over the extra US$6 to travel in greater luxury, but if you're up for the adventure, traveling like a local can be a great way to stretch your funds and add more color to your memories.

FUN FACT

The two-day journey from Thailand to Laos, along the Mekong River, features bus seats on its slow boat.

Kim

One summer I found myself staying at an independent hostel overlooking a private vineyard in Parma, Italy. The hostel was situated a little more than halfway up a hillside just outside the city center. Unfortunately for me, it wasn't walkable into town and required taking the local bus to get around. Contrary to my understanding of buses, this one didn't stop at every stop automatically. Instead, the locals would pull a string that ran along the top of the inside of the bus that would chime a bell alerting the driver they wanted to be dropped off at the upcoming stop.

After a few days of finding myself the last passenger (and only non-local) at the top of the mountain, never successfully discerning which stop was mine on the tree-lined mountain road, I braved the bell, finally believing I knew where my stop was located. I was wrong. So much of traveling is faking confidence until you actually have it. When the driver came to a stop, I knew it wasn't the right stop, but instead of shrinking back to my seat and waiting to be chauffeured from the top of the mountain, I marched off and started schlepping it up the mountain road. In an attempt to make lemonade out of lemons, I mentally embraced the mishap as a way to experience a secluded Italian hillside all by myself. That was until the rain started.

After you've traveled for any length of time, you'll discover that there are people we'll dub "road angels" who enter your life at exactly the right moment. They are strangers with good intentions and a helpful heart that seemingly appear just when you've given up hope that your situation will resolve itself on its own. This was the first time I was helped by a road angel. A man driving home pulled up next to me slogging my way up the hillside in the rain, offering me a lift to the hostel. At that moment, several thoughts were in my mind, namely safety and convenience. I had a decision to make. Do I get in the car and trust this stranger will safely deliver me to my hostel or turn down the offer and hike for however much longer, not really knowing where I was? Fortunately, my instincts were correct and I'm able to share this account with you here, for it could just as easily have gone a different way.

It's important to listen to and hone your instincts so you can be prepared when help arrives. It may not always be obvious, and you may not need to accept it, but there's a certain level of trust required that the Universe will provide if you are able to step outside what you know and brave the raindrops.

Long-Haul "Tourist" Busses

Don't be put off by the idea of taking a long-haul "tourist" bus. In many low-income countries, the tourist bus is synonymous with air conditioning, comfort, and a noticeable absence of chickens. If you are planning to travel throughout a given country, it is worth exploring these options as they travel daily (if not more frequently) between major hubs within the country without stopping to let people on and off every few minutes. You can rest easy on these long rides knowing that you will be awoken upon arrival at your destination.

Tickets for tourist buses can often be purchased from your accommodation, local travel agents, or directly from the bus operator. In the high seasons, it's not uncommon for these buses to sell out, so it is always worth inquiring about tickets prior to the day you would like to travel. We advise that if you have to make any flights, trains, important events, or connecting travel, that you always allow an extra day as a buffer.

Natasha

Note that many countries within Africa have a reputation for buses departing at their own leisure. In Malawi, I rushed to catch a 10:00 a.m. bus only to find out that it would not leave until all the seats were sold and filled. As a result, the bus did not leave until nearly 1:00 p.m.

SOME SAFETY ADVICE

- Figure out your ticket cost in advance and try to have exact change in hand (don't pull out wads of cash)
- Double-check that you are going to the correct place—ask the driver or a local
- If you must wait, sit or stand in a well-lit area with other travelers or locals
- Do not leave your belongings unattended, even to use the bathroom
- If you're alone and feeling uncomfortable, find a family or couple and ask if you can wait with them or sit near them on the bus

Boats

Love small spaces and being rocked to sleep by ocean waves? Well, there is a really cool subgroup of backpackers who are sailing the world. There're a few ways to approach this, whether you pay for your lodging, volunteer for free or, if you're so inclined, even turn your love of travel and adventure into a paid career. We'll touch on a few below.

Crewing on Ships & Yachts

During our travels through port towns around Southeast Asia and Australia, it was not uncommon to chat with travelers who were in town for a few nights restocking necessary items for their next voyage at sea.

Experience is not always necessary, so if you have unique skills or prior experience, be sure to emphasize these attributes to make yourself a more valuable consideration. You should be prepared to talk knowledgeably and present yourself accordingly. Remember, this is a career option for many people, therefore be respectful in your solicitation.

There are many sites with useful information on how to enter the world of crewing. We'll include some links in the appendix. Whichever route you decide, be it walking down to the docks, connecting with a cool captain, or using one of the helpful links provided at the end of the book, this is an incredible way to travel the world.

Kim

I met several backpackers during my stay in Manly, Australia, who were sailing to South Africa. Through further investigation, I learned that many of them came into their current aquatic adventures by simply putting on some nice clothes, walking down to the local docks, and chatting with the yachties and local crews to inquire if any work might be available. Apparently, you can even just hitch a ride for the day and return to port that night. I learned it's not uncommon to receive an invitation to sail the high seas after a good chat and a few highballs of rum.

Freight Ships & Ferries

If you find yourself near a port town and like the idea of a cruise but want something a little more unique, consider traveling to your next destination by freight ship. These are generally less explored options that offer unique experiences to the traveler who really is about the adventure and has time on their side.

The plainest advice would be to ask around at your hostel then head down to the docks and inquire if any freight ships are accepting volunteer passengers. You may be required to assist in day-to-day activities or pay a nominal fee. Be sure to be clear in your intention when discussing your options. The idea here is to be a volunteer deckhand rather than a stowaway and not treat the experience like you might a cruise ship.

Traveling by freight ship is an option not only around Europe but also in more remote locations, such as the outer islands of the Philippines. While it can be significantly cheaper than flights, it will require more time and flexibility.

Ferries, on the other hand, are great options for exploring more remote islands and byways away from the coastal mainland. Whether you're transporting your vehicle or are just a passenger along for the ride, they're cheap, can offer great photo opportunities, and sometimes even dolphin sightings! Be sure to check the ferry schedule in advance to confirm they're operating. There's nothing like driving 100 miles out of the way to take a ferry crossing only to learn they've closed the route until the next spring.

> **PRO-TIP**
> In a 2009 blog post, Joseph P. Lenze wrote about his experiences and travel tips for anyone interested in venturing abroad by way of the mighty seas. Check out his online article How to Cross the Ocean on a Freighter Ship at The Art of Manliness.

Tuk-Tuks

Tuk-Tuk is the onomatopoeic slang and most commonly heard name used for auto-rickshaws. The name stems from mimicking the sound of their engines. They are a strange but affordable form of urban transportation seen predominantly throughout Asia. The look will vary by region, but they are primarily a motorcycle with a small, covered seating area behind or beside the driver. It is usually a tight fit accommodating one to three passengers, but significantly cheaper than a taxi.

Unless instructed otherwise by a local, it is common to negotiate pricing. Be sure to agree on a price prior to entering the vehicle with no exception. Some drivers may try to hurry you into the vehicle as a way of pressuring or tricking you into paying an exorbitant fee. The only way to prevent this is to be firm that you will not enter the vehicle until a price has been agreed upon.

If you are taking a tuk-tuk to a remote location such as a hidden beach or temple, consult with your hostel beforehand about what transportation options you will have for your return. On occasion your tuk-tuk driver will be your only option and you should negotiate a price for him to return or wait for you. Arranging a return price prior to departing is also prudent as to not leave you stranded or price gouged as a result. Riding in a tuk-tuk is almost a rite of passage when exploring Asia.

Embrace the chaos and enjoy the ride!!!

Wooden Canoes

When traveling through remote areas of Asia, Central, or South America, you are likely to encounter wooden canoes as passage to smaller islands. We can tell you from experience that if the only means to get from point A to point B is a local fisherman you can barely understand and a boat that slowly takes on water—you are in for a treat! A couple of favorite obscure, canoe-worthy destinations are Don Det (Four Thousand Islands), Laos, and the caves of Lago Bayano in Panama.

Bicycle

There are many countries where the most accepted and standard form of transportation is a bicycle, including but not limited to northern European countries such as the Netherlands, Denmark, Norway, Sweden, and Germany.

Motorbikes

If you're comfortable riding or eager to learn, then traveling by motorbike, Vespa, or scooter are obvious considerations for countries such as Italy, Vietnam, China, India, and regions such as Central and South America. Ride Expeditions, a British-owned company, organizes adventure tours all around the world and comes highly recommended.

Kim

I once met a mother and son in a Paris hostel who were cycling around Europe as an opportunity to spend time together before he went off to university. This was gleaned after noticing each had a single wheel neatly stacked with their limited gear, beside their adjoining bunk beds in the hostel room we were sharing. So cool!

Horseback, Camel & Dogsled

There are many incredible places on this great planet to explore your surroundings via quadruped. Check out the local tourist office or hostel listings for private companies offering self- or guided horseback, camelback, or dogsled tours.

Natasha

When you arrive in the backpacker hubs of Thailand, be it Khao San Road, Phuket, Chiang Mai, or especially Pai, you will immediately notice all the young travelers have one thing in common...gauze bandages! I'm not even exaggerating, something like one in five backpackers will have a distinct gauze bandage wrapped around a limb or joint. Bonus points if this is combined with a corresponding limp. Plenty are due to the ridiculous beach party festivities: fire poi, flaming limbo, or the most insane fire jump rope (don't even get me started on this one). However, the number one culprit is motorbike accidents, and these accidents are so prevalent that locals and backpackers alike have taken to charmingly referring to such injuries and scars as "Thai Tattoos." Even I have donned a few Thai Tattoos.

The rainy season's muddy and winding roads, combined with motorbike rentals requiring zero experience, provides never-ending hospital subsidies from overconfident backpackers. I won't deny this mode of transportation is one of the best ways to explore off the beaten path. I also won't deny the truly hypnotic, wind-enhaced experience of riding on the back of a new lover's motorcycle. Just please, please, please ride safely and, for the love of all things holy, wear a helmet.

Natasha

One evening in Ushuaia, Argentina (southernmost tip of South America/Patagonia), I embarked on a dogsled excursion. Initially, I was picked up by snow mobile for the 40-minute journey into the Tierra del Fuego National Park. Once there, I was handed a pair of snowshoes (quite the novelty for a Floridian) to trek through the snowy valley while watching the sunset over the mountains. After the trek, we set up camp in the forest in an enormous domed tent with a hole in the top to allow for smoke release (commonly referred to as a yurt). There, the group drank hot mulled wine, ate rustic Argentinian BBQ, and sang along with the Spanish guitar by the campfire. Not one person spoke a word of English and I still felt right at home. Once our meal was complete, we went outside to see dozens of huskies raring to go with sleds behind them. We each climbed on as the "mushers" signaled the dogs to action. The speed stunned me as the cold wind smacked my face, and the huskies howled as they slalomed down the torch-lit path in the snowy forest until we arrived at a vast clearing under the stars. It was an experience and feeling I have been unable to ever replicate again. I can't promise every dogsled adventure will be as remarkable, but I can promise it's worth a try.

Walking, Hiking & Trekking

If you've signed on to travel, you've signed on to walk. Make sure the shoes you leave home with are comfortable and able to sustain your pending epic adventures. However, we feel it necessary to include walking as its own category beyond the scope of a city walking tour (which we highly recommend) or just ambling along between cafes, museums, and bars. Depending on where you are, walking tours, treks, and hikes will be available and cater to all levels of fitness or capability; simply inquire at your hostel.

Kim

Journal entry, Reflections on walking 500 miles across northern Spain

"It's like a drug, or so people say. I don't know if I'd consider myself addicted (yet), but there are certainly highs, lows, pain, withdrawal, euphoria, and a certain degree of submission that comes with walking the Camino de Santiago de Compostela. Today is my 11th day on the Camino, having begun this journey on the 27th of June. I began from St. Jean-Pied-de-Port, France, and am currently writing to you from a small village in Spain, between Grañón (where I stayed last night) and Tosantos (where I intend to stay tonight). I average about 20 kilometers a day, give or take, but yesterday I walked 39 kilometers! To put it into perspective, that's just shy of 25 miles. I can't say, either, why I walked so far—there is a lot about the Camino that I simply can't explain.

"I can say that this isn't what I expected, although I can't honestly say I came with any real expectations. I find this journey a constant contradiction. In no way would I say the walk is overly difficult and yet it is certainly not easy. I keep hoping or intending for great insight to pop into my head, but of course at these moments, there is nothing. At other times, say when attending a mass (I've attended more church services in the last ten days than in the last ten years combined), specific and detailed thoughts come into my mind outlining how I intend to realize my dream of owning a New Zealand hostel.

"I'm often surprised at the relationships that develop along the way and yet how there can be days where no connections are made at all. Some days I find myself pulling back into myself, →

wanting to yell at those walking nearby to 'shut up, can't you see I'm trying to be reflective here?!' Then there are other times where I welcome the communication, insight, philosophies, and human connection. In this respect, the Camino is always giving and taking away.

"I've stayed at some very interesting albergues (hostels) pronounced al-BEAR-gays, some more special than others. I was given a list of recommended albergues to try and visit and have not once been disappointed. Sometimes the hostels are just like you'd find anywhere else where for a fee you receive a bed (no sheets—had to buy a sleeping bag), shower, and maybe there is a kitchen or a bar to buy food. Other times I've been blessed to find really nice hostels that are based on donations, providing a full three-course dinner and breakfast in the morning. Last night, in Grañón, was such an occasion.

"Most mornings, I am up and walking out the door by 6:30 a.m., usually covering 20 kilometers by 11:00 a.m. (including a break for coffee). Today I have decided to take things slowly. I often find I have to remind myself to slow down. There is a pace on the Camino...three lanes of traffic if you will. There are those in the slow lane, that start from far away, often in central France or even as far as Holland and have already been on the road for over a month by the time I meet them...they are taking their time. Then there are those in the fast-passing lane, who have either limited time to walk or who wish to make it to Santiago de Compostela by the 25th of July (big festival) and are go-go-go!!! Then there's everyone else (myself included), who sort of weave in and out of traffic with no real hurry to finish, but a deadline all the same. Sometimes I even ponder if finishing is the ultimate goal...and yet, after a day like yesterday where my body literally felt broken, today I wake to find my body and legs feeling stronger than on any day since beginning. If that wasn't enough, then a farmer takes time to stop, shake my hand, kiss me on each cheek, and wish me well on my way. Then my spirit is renewed, and I am reminded of why I came and that I can really do this."

How to Travel for One Year or Longer...

Embracing the "Gap Year"
noun | British

A period, typically an academic year, taken by a student as a break between secondary school and higher education. Alternatively, this year may be taken upon completion of higher education and before initiation of career trajectory.

Study Abroad!

Every day we were abroad, we met students from all over the world studying, well, all over the world! Literally, make the world your classroom.

Natasha Study Abroad, Part One

There came a point in my life where I desperately wanted to continue my education but couldn't bare the idea of giving up life on the road to stay in one place semester after semester just yet. I wracked my brain with how I could combine both of these elements of my life. Over time I realized that a degree in anthropology would be best suited to my interests and possibly integrate elements of travel. I re-enrolled at my university and started signing up for classes. It was the early days of online learning with only a few scattered options available at my university, but the idea stuck in the back of my mind.

As the start of the semester grew closer two pivotal things happened:

1. I qualified for a grant to cover living expenses
2. My anxiety to put down a deposit on an apartment haunted me.

One anxious night the solution came to me. Ask each of my professors to let me do all my course work online. These were well-traveled academics teaching about cultures of the world after all, and the worst that could happen is they say no.

I practiced my pitch for days before visiting the office hours of each possible professor. The first said, "No, forensics is practical and requires hands on training." Sure, that makes sense. The second professor said, "Hmmm, let me have a think about it and get back to you." Okay, a little progress. The third professor wasn't even in their office. Finally, the professor I had been waiting for: "You know, that sounds like an incredible idea! It's going to be a lot of work on your part, and I may have to assign you additional assignments to make up for the classroom time, but I think we can make something work." Hallelujah! With her help I was able to come up with a hybrid program with four separate professors. There were some that required video call oral exams, some that required extra written assignments, some that uploaded their lectures online for me, and others who said it was on me to find a way to get all the materials from other students but that

I could email my papers. This was going to happen!

I went home and excitedly told my friends and family — I was obscenely proud of myself. Unfortunately, the reactions varied on a scale between skeptical to downright telling me I was going to fail. As annoyed as I was by their reactions at the time, it motivated me to prove them wrong. I mapped out how to stretch my financial stipend to fund a year traveling though Asia. Knowing there was no way I could carry all my textbooks in my pack, I found a new tablet and downloaded all the pdfs. I meticulously mapped out every single assignment in a checklist in my calendar and hit the road. The coming months proved to be some of the most challenging and inspiring of my life.

I can't say there weren't challenges - finding quality Wi-Fi in rural Asia proved challenging (but not impossible), the time difference meant that many of my oral exams had to take place in the middle of the night, and it was incredibly difficult to abstain from some incredible excursions when I needed to study. →

However, on the other side there were incredible moments:

- While taking an online exam on a beach outside my hostel at 2:00 a.m. in the Philippines (as it was the only place the Wi-Fi was strong enough to allow for a video call), a few backpackers I befriended drunkenly stopped by my exam to cheer me on and motivate me with a coconut water and lemon pancake.
- When I needed to study throughout the fourteen-hour bus ride on the winding mountain roads of Nepal, but kept getting too car sick to study, a fellow backpacker came to my aid and read my textbook aloud for me.
- In Singapore, where I sat studying outside the twenty-four-hour Indian cafe all night (again with the time difference issue) and the owner watched over me and brought a never-ending supply of snacks "on the house" because he was so proud of a young woman working so hard and hoped that someone would do the same for his daughter one day.
- During the time I was studying in Malawi and heavy rain fell to the point of a regional flooding disaster. Through a series of events, I was able to assist international aid agencies with their relief efforts.

In the end I landed with a nearly perfect average and a renewed sense of possibility in the world. I repeated this process semester after semester (though I did have to return home to make up my forensics course before I could graduate) and while it took me nearly eight years to complete my four-year degree, I can't imagine a better way to have spent those years of my life.

Study Abroad, Part Two

As I neared the ripe old age of thirty (eye roll), the travel/work youth visas began to dry up. With the desire to both to live abroad in one country for an extended time and continue my education, I applied for a master's program in the UK. Six months later I was a resident and full-time student in London. Studying in Europe was not only a fraction of the cost of most universities in the United States but allowed me to take advantage of countless trains and Easy Jet flights all over the continent. I even meet my future husband on the streets of London.

These educational oversees experiences opened the doors for me to do work for foreign embassies and land a job at one of the largest international development agencies in the world. I am forever thankful for my decision to study abroad!

Teach English or Another Language Overseas

A quick online search will yield many overseas foreign language service options. Be sure to fully read the contract and commitment requirements. These are often one-year contracts in rural locations. Keep in mind, these are jobs and professionalism and commitment are required. The incentive is you'll have an opportunity to do a deep dive into a region and live and work among locals. It can be truly rewarding and yield continued opportunities when your posting is complete.

Volunteer

If you're considering a more immersive international experience where you can leave the planet a little better than how you found it (we believe this should be an everyday effort), then consider connecting with an organization that offers overseas volunteer opportunities.

PRO-TIP

If volunteering abroad is something you're considering, please be sure to research the ethical standards of any organization you are considering, ensuring the service you're looking to supply isn't actually doing more (long-term) harm than good. Volunteering and voluntourism may seem like synonyms, but they have starkly different definitions that you should learn and present different questions you should ask. Take your time in researching to discern the appropriate questions to ask in order to determine if this is a volunteer organization that you can not only feel good about supporting but feel safe with in a foreign (and in many cases remote) country.

The first Full Moon Party is said to have been improvised at a Paradise Bungalows on the beach in 1983 as a token of thanks to about 20—30 travelers. The parties gained fame through word of mouth, and the event now draws a crowd of about 5,000—30,000 every full moon evening. The modern event has become a part of the itinerary of many travelers to Southeast Asia.

10 Bucket List Ideas

To check off your list

21. Buy a car and camp around Western Australia................ ☐
22. Forget your name at a Full Moon Party in Thailand.......... ☐
23. Marvel at the midnight sun above the Arctic Circle......... ☐
24. Eat an edible in the Red-Light District, Amsterdam......... ☐
25. Sit in a thermal pool in the Coromandel, New Zealand....... ☐
26. Take a motorcycle tour through Nepal....................... ☐
27. Walk on a glacier in Iceland or New Zealand................ ☐
28. Explore Mayan ruins in South America...................... ☐
29. Dance your face off at Tomorrowland EDM Festival in Boom, Belgium ☐
30. Hail a classic 1950s cab in Cuba........................... ☐

4

SOMETIMES YOU'RE STUCK

TOSS YOUR ITINERARY AND GO WITH THE FLOW

Never let a rigid itinerary discourage you from an unexpected adventure.
—Josiah Bancroft, Senlin Ascends

Sometimes, despite your best laid plans, the Universe has something entirely different planned for you to experience, contrary to what you meticulously planned. What may appear to be a setback or an inconvenience might actually be an opportunity to slow down, savor, and enjoy a location, or even a person, at a slower than breakneck pace. Sometimes itinerary mishaps result from poor personal planning, including destination miscalculations, staying out too late, being hungover, or oversleeping. Maybe you simply over- or undershot your transit stop, creating a tighter timetable to get to your next destination; maybe you altogether end up missing a departure or connection. Both of us have been there and missed flights, ferries, buses, and trains for all of the above reasons mentioned, more than once.

Other situations are completely out of your control, and no amount of planning could have changed the outcome. These include hotel worker and transit strikes, vehicle breakdowns, natural disasters, and bank holidays that can prevent currency exchange when you don't have or can't use a debit or credit card. Even with all the conveniences of technology and money transfer apps, some places still only take cash!

Embarrassingly enough, on more than one occasion we've each misplaced or left (in a safe) our passports and had to backtrack to retrieve them. Just to be clear, realizing you don't have your passport is one of the worst-case scenarios you can find yourself in. If you lose it drunk at a bar, in a cab, at a hostel, or at the house of that random person who let you crash, you must move heaven and earth to recover it, otherwise you'll seriously be stuck, and it won't be an easy fix to wedge yourself out of. Once again, make copies of your important documents, carry a copy in your pack and leave a set with a trusted friend or family member back home as well as digitally on your phone, a flash stick, or on a cloud drive.

There are plenty of other, less harrowing, reasons you may feel stuck along the way. Maybe you joined a tour and aren't resonating with the group or guide. Similarly, you might acquire a travel companion who you just aren't clicking with, but you can't quite break away from them yet. ➜

Of course, if you're feeling uncomfortable or scared to be somewhere or around someone, then it's time to get immediately unstuck and safely get the hell out of the situation!

More often than not, each of these experiences will yield an interesting lesson, even if only in hindsight. Before jumping ship and going it alone again, journal your feelings and try to find the beauty in the experience, even if it's just for another day.

We've both been there, running flat out down an airport concourse, praying our flip-flops (thongs for our Aussie friends) don't fly off, dodging the motorized trolley carrying grandmothers from their terminals, backpacks jostling hard enough to make us fall during our desperate sprint to arrive at the gate on time even though we've already heard our name announced over the loudspeaker for final boarding, knowing we're not going to make it before they lock the door! Yeah, that's a bummer.

Maybe you'll find yourself in Europe, working your way up from Florence to Frankfurt am Main with connections in Milan and Bern. There are so many scenarios here where your plans can get derailed, from delays at border crossings to arrival or departure delays at changeover stations, the list goes on. You get the idea.

If you find yourself experiencing something similar, take a deep breath, wish the travelers that made it onward a safe trip, grab a cup of coffee or your journal, and regroup. Once you've calmed down, remember there will always be another flight, bus, ferry, train, etc. It's worth budgeting for these situations—if not financially, then definitely mentally—and if you end up having to stay another night, make it count! Do something uniquely local and fun. If time is of the essence, however, and you can get out later that same day, journal or blog about your experience while you're waiting. These are the moments you will want to read back on later when you find yourself home and dreaming of your next adventure.

Remember, you're a traveler and it's all part of the greater story of your life. Give yourself a written affirmation to one day go back and read with pride and confidence about your ability to navigate challenging and unforeseen situations in a foreign country. If it ever feels overwhelming, write an affirmation on the inside cover of your travel journal to read when times get tough:

I am Brave. I am Curious. I am Resourceful. I've got this!

PRO-TIP

Give yourself extra time to allow for delays or even getting lost along your way. Try not to sweat the interruptions to your schedule. Remind yourself how brave you are for being there in the first place and just how amazing that simple act is in itself.

Kim

Upon leaving the Abel Tasman National Park on the South Island of New Zealand, my 1984 red Mitsubishi Sigma GSR-X Turbo, posthumously named Morning View (after the bootleg cassette tape discovered in the glove compartment), decided we were finished traveling together and that I should find alternative means.

Apparently, Morning View's previous backpacker owner, who had applied for the required warrant of fitness (WoF) sticker, didn't realize the mechanic had attached a radiator hose that was too large. Due to jostling from the varied terrain across the islands, the hose had bunched up and pressure had been building, until eventually the radiator hose blew off (again) and damaged the head gasket, which caused oil to leak into the car's coolant. During a come-to-Jesus conversation with the repair shop, I was informed the car was worth more as scrap than it was worth investing in repairs, so Morning View and I parted ways.

Foolishly, after about a month together, I had stopped thinking minimally (essentially only purchasing what I could pack in my bag and comfortably carry) and had started to acquire larger mementos, bottles of wine, etc. I could not have predicted I would have to pack and ship my souvenirs so soon and be back to bussing, hitchhiking, riding trains, and relying on the generosity of other backpackers.

Purchasing Morning View was still the absolute best decision I made in New Zealand, and in hindsight, I wish I'd had the foresight to do so in Australia. It afforded me flexibility, the ability to see things at a leisurely pace, camp, witness sunsets and sunrises, talk long into the night with my new travel companion, and prove I was capable (at twenty-two years old) of making decisions and accepting those responsibilities without any familial assistance, alone, on the other side of the world. While I lost money and time in the process, the confidence I gained as well as the life-long friend that I met and traveled with as a result would have me do it exactly the same way again!

Scenarios That Might Slow Your Roll

Vehicle Breakdowns
Personal or tour vehicles of all varieties get a lot of mileage and wear and tear put on them over the seasons. Take these setbacks in stride and know you'll be on your way again, one way or another.

Transit & Rail Delays
This can include delays at border control crossings where passport checks are required, possibly impacting your arrival or connection schedule. In Europe many of the InterCity Express (ICE) rail lines—the really high-speed ones—will stop mid-journey on the tracks to allow a train coming from the opposite direction to safely pass at such a high speed. Though unlikely, a mid-journey pause can impact timed connections, especially if you're on a tight schedule.

Missing Your Connection (Flight, Train, Bus, Ferry)
Sometimes the Universe is asking you to slow down (see above) and other times it's your own damn fault. Regardless of the reason, missing your connecting flight, train, or bus isn't awesome. It's also not the end of the world, so use honey rather than vinegar when asking for assistance making flight or transit changes. Even if you're completely frazzled, remember the people who can help troubleshoot the situation will either be your friend or foe. Exhibiting kindness, even when you're the most stressed out, will yield a more encouraging outcome than if you are rude and spit acid. Sometimes this approach can even yield a more favorable ticket time or more direct transit option than you may have originally been able to afford.

Get comfortable! Sometimes there's nothing that can be done, and you can't be on your way for another day or two. In these instances, it's best to find a comfortable place to stay, grab a cuppa, and journal about the experience. You'll look back on it as a good story even if it may not feel like it at the moment.

Skipping your Connection

Sometimes you want to be stuck somewhere longer, and if your budget allows or there's not a huge financial penalty to changing your flight (such as in purchasing an Around the World ticket), consider skipping your connection instead. For a change fee of about US$100, sometimes it's worth skipping your connection to afford you an opportunity to explore a place that wasn't originally on your travel itinerary. Remember, you're in charge of your destiny and no one is holding you to the plans you left home with. Plans change. Go forward in that knowledge feeling confident. Embrace the unexpected and unknown; it's what traveling is all about!

Bank Holidays

These closures can have a unique impact on your experience, especially if you're traveling with traveler's checks or need to exchange foreign currency from one country to another. Not everyone lives and dies by their credit or debit cards, and for the budget-savvy traveler, a bank offers a much more favorable exchange of currency than an ATM.

Strikes

Workforce strikes are more common outside the United States, especially transit union strikes. These can happen seemingly without warning and, unless you're paying close attention to the local news or politics for the region you're currently traveling in, can downright thwart your timetable for getting around. Generally speaking, at least in Europe, they resolve rather quickly and only last a few days to a week.

If you have the time, consider these delays, setbacks, or pauses as little gifts bestowed on you to really get to know the location you're in more intimately. Walk around and enjoy popping in and out of places at a slower pace. Pick up a book at your hostel and find a park to read in. Pretend you're a local for a day.

If you must move on—perhaps you have a big day of travel the next day—speak with the proprietor of your hostel, hotel, or Airbnb and see if they can offer assistance or know of any other travelers who may also need to leave. You'll be surprised how helpful complete strangers in foreign countries can be when you really need it. Road angels are real.

PRO-TIP

Always check what terminal from which you are departing! In some airports the terminals are not connected within the airport and require a taxi to transport you from one terminal to the next. In these cases, it is not uncommon for taxi drivers to take advantage of the situation (i.e, you have gone to the wrong terminal and only have X-amount of time to get to the correct terminal to catch your flight) and inflate the cost of the fare.

Protests

While generally peaceful, protests can disrupt all sorts of plans including travel into, around, or between destinations. If protests are peaceful, this is a unique opportunity to be a cultural fly on the wall. While you may understand the strife that affects you at home, bearing witness to how other countries approach freedom of speech and expression is a rather unique opportunity. Above all, be safe and try not to be in a hurry. Roads may be closed and rideshares, taxis, buses, or trains might be unavailable, unaffordable, delayed, or altogether canceled because of the protest. We recommend not participating after dark. Nothing good will come of that.

Natasha

I have been stuck more than I care to admit. Heavy rains blocking roads and flat tires in Luang Prabang, Laos. A workers' strike in Crete, Greece. An air traffic controllers' strike in Athens. A government protest in Bangkok. Even the Arab Spring demonstrations while I was visiting Cairo, Egypt. If I had known that any of these would have happened ahead of time, I would likely have been quite scared, and probably even cancelled my trip. I will never encourage anyone to seek out such experiences as you never know when they can turn dangerous. However, I can say without a shadow of a doubt that each of these experiences turned into incredible, unique adventures.

In Laos, the flat tire of the vehicle left a group of us to party with the locals in a rural village. In Crete, I found myself stuck in the city center as a local Greek party broke out with tons of pastries and ouzo provided. In Athens, I was able to extend my trip by four days at no cost to me as the airline was required to rebook my trip. In Bangkok, I watched democracy in action before my very eyes. And while the Arab Spring has lasting impacts on the wider world, for me it meant that I was able to visit the Pyramids of Giza with only a small handful of other visitors present.

Getting stuck can be stressful, but instead of wasting your time frustrated in the airport, bus station, etc. try to embrace the experience. It might be the most memorable one yet.

Illness

Depending on the severity, being sick can keep you from moving on to the next location. This can be as simple as a common cold to more-severe allergic reactions. Outside of the US, most pharmacies or chemists can prescribe over-the-counter antibiotics, anti-nausea, or pain meds to tackle most ailments that will try to slow you down.

Kim

While traveling the South Island of New Zealand, I found myself pain ridden, curled up in a youth hostel, battling a goopy bout of conjunctivitis that had turned in to a gnarly sinus infection. Knowing I had a full day of travel ahead of me, I made my way to the local pharmacy for a second time. When I met with the doctor, he noted the severity of my infection and asked, "When do you plan to travel?"

I responded, "Tomorrow." In fact, I had a minimum of fourteen hours of travel — with three plane transfers and two layovers — starting at 6:00 a.m. The response I received in return was a memorable one. After pausing a beat, the doctor replied, "Are you fucking kidding me?" I was not. Needless to say, you don't want to wait to treat that sinus infection until the day before your next flight and risk rupturing your ear drums upon take off. Speaking from personal experience, this is painful, scary, and avoidable!

Allergies or Severe Ailments

If you suffer from severe allergies or a monitored ailment, it's your responsibility to travel with the proper documented medications or treatments. Be in control of your health and know where to go or who to reach out to for help if you need it.

Hospitals: In more severe or serious situations, you may need to go to a hospital. Don't wait or avoid seeking treatment because you think you can't afford it. Like we've said, in many foreign countries hospital treatment is afforded to all and you may not pay anything beyond a pharmacy script; however, should you break your leg while heli-skiing in the Swiss Alps, you will be glad you took out some travel insurance. You just never know.

> **PRO-TIP**
>
> Speaking of the unpredictable, no one could have anticipated the impact COVID-19 would have on the world. Both of us had international trips planned in early 2020 that required cancelation or rescheduling. We were independently informed that most airlines and travel companies were requiring proof of (already purchased) travel insurance for all refund requests per their cancellation policies—during a pandemic! Keep this in mind if you're booking a tour, multileg flight series, rail passes, and hostels in advance. Read the fine print of their cancellation policies to see if securing some amount of travel insurance makes sense. The unexpected happens a lot more than you think when you're traveling; make sure you can still enjoy your experience when it does.

A Note on Traveler's Health Insurance and Seeking Medical Attention Abroad:

The United States has one of the most expensive healthcare systems of any country, so it would be reasonable for an American backpacker to weigh the pros and cons of purchasing travel health insurance before heading abroad. We've both purchased and not purchased it depending on the destination country, length of time away, and wanting to feel more secure should an emergency arise. If you are a foreigner visiting the United States, we strongly suggest purchasing travel health insurance for the peace of mind that you will both receive the care you need and be able to afford the bill presented upon exiting.

If you are from the US and get sick abroad, you may hesitate to seek medical attention out of fear of the potential costs associated with even the most routine exam. This is understandable, however, as we've both discovered, with rare exceptions, seeking healthcare abroad can be very affordable (even for a backpacker) – possibly even free in some cases. If you don't know where the wind will blow you on your travels, or plan to spend the entire time bouncing from one extreme activity to another, certainly consider purchasing travel health insurance. Some credit cards even offer built-in travel protection as part of their annual fee expense. At the end of the day, consider this decision a break glass in case of emergency purchase – you likely won't need it but may end up glad you have it. If you're only traveling for a short period of time, do not have any underlying health considerations, and are currently in great health, then maybe this is a purchase you can consider putting off. We can't speak for you. Sometimes, it's just about the peace of mind. Stay healthy out there!

Natural or Man-made Disasters

If you are traveling with a phone, leave the Find My Phone setting on so technology can be utilized to locate you in the event of an emergency. This could mean being lost in the woods at the top of a mountain or being caught up in a riot and stranded in a strange city. Both examples are avoidable, therefore stay curious but don't be reckless!

It is important to know the location of your embassy and how to contact it, including:

* Physical address
* Telephone number
* Website/Email contact

In summary and maybe most importantly, tell someone back home where you plan to be. Updating your family or friends with a short email about where you intend to be next and for how long can be enough information for them to follow up if the unthinkable happens. Assume those following your travels back home will be glued to the news and all things happening in the areas and regions you'll travel through. It takes very little effort to send a quick note and doesn't let them worry unnecessarily.

Kim

I don't really recall what drove me to purchase a plane ticket to Mongolia. I think in part it was because I'd spent the better part of a year and a half backpacking in extremely Western, Anglo-Saxon countries despite my best intention to complete the Southeast Asia backpacker circuit after leaving Australia and New Zealand. Similar to the coronavirus pandemic of 2020, years ago China experienced a viral coronavirus outbreak (SARS) that rapidly spread to twenty—

six countries, infecting a little more than eight thousand people and killing just under eight hundred. While on a much smaller scale compared to 2020, US news outlets were reporting on the illness and cautioning those traveling through infected areas to wear masks or altogether avoid those areas to be safe.

It's really difficult to reassure those back home who love you and are worried for you that all is well, and you are in fact safe in the decisions you're making, especially when (at the time) the fear of a worldwide outbreak was deemed imminent. While I always trusted my instincts, I valued my parents' concerns, checked in with them regularly, and applied extra precaution out of respect more often than was always necessary. It was for this reason that I did not intentionally miss my connecting flight from Kuala Lumpur to London as I'd originally intended. In my mind, I'd get back there sooner rather than later, which was an acceptable concession at the time.

At the time Mongolia felt like the most non-Western, non-gentrified, remote experience I could wrap my hands around, and I wanted to prove (to myself) that I could do it! After all, I was now a seasoned traveler, and after only one year back at home, my twenty-four-year-old self was ready for the next adventure, so why not make it a remote one? The trouble with picking far-out places is you don't always know how—let alone where—to start your research. Today the world is so connected that the options seem endlessly available, which at the time was not the case. Sure, backpacking Europe was outlined in great detail in every travel section of my local bookstores, but backpacking around Mongolia was not. The flip side to being able to easily source all the information you could ever want or need is that you miss out on the accidental adventures or simple dumb luck situations you'd otherwise experience in figuring it out without all the information at your fingertips.

At the end of the day, despite all my newly gained confidence on the road, I wasn't so sure about simply showing up at the airport in Ulaanbaatar (capital city of Mongolia) and just winging it like I had throughout Europe, Australia, and New Zealand in prior years. I felt like, this time, I needed to map some things out and leave with a proper plan, so I booked a fourteen-day adventure tour. I figured if I was going to be on someone else's time schedule and itinerary, I may as well get to ride some camels in the Gobi while I was at it.

I don't recall all the details of how I arrived except instead of being routed through China (for which I'd obtained a visa for my flight connection), I ended up connecting in Seoul, South Korea. Notably, what stands out was when the plane deboarded, instead of filing out one row at a time, every other side of the aisle, everyone just shot up out of their seats and shoved to the front of the plane, mere millimeters from one another. This simple cultural divergence from the perceived civility of our Western ways was my first introduction to the wide-ranging cultural differences I'd encounter. At the time it felt impolite, but I quickly learned that personal space didn't hold the same meaning everywhere →

in this world and being assertive (or even downright pushy) in securing your place in line isn't necessarily considered rude.

The moment I arrived at the Buyant-Ukhaa International Airport, I knew instinctively that I could have traveled through this country alone. This said, I was glad for the opportunities to ensure I didn't miss out on any of the country-specific highlights I might otherwise have missed. What I struggled with then (and still do now) was adhering to someone else's itinerary and being on someone else's timeline. During my year and a half of adventures, I had set, kept, managed, and mismanaged my own timeline and was very accustomed to honoring decisions made in the moment. This two-week organized tour thing was going to be a challenge.

My time in Mongolia was a constant internal battle of wills for me. Let me explain—I'm an only child and independent to a fault. Just ask my father, husband, and every ex-boyfriend, they'll all confirm it's true. Truthfully speaking, I don't always want to be hyper-independent but this constant struggle to hand over the reins is something that has proven easier said than done over the years. If I'm honest, it's genuinely kept me from fully enjoying experiences in the moment because I'm too bullheaded to resign or appreciate the simplicity in enjoying what I'm experiencing.

For this reason, I often questioned if how I was traveling or experiencing the world was the wrong way if I wasn't creating every circumstance from scratch, so to speak. As if joining a tour, where the hard work (the scrappiness in figuring out the unknown and the planning) was taken care of, was in some way cheating.

I dwelled in this internal conflict instead of being out of my mind and stoked that I was in fucking Mongolia!! Because of this I made myself righteously sick! In part it was probably something I ate or drank combined with a propensity for being motion sick (I enjoyed my most epic projectile vomiting experience on a hopper flight leaving the Gobi) but the truth is, I was also doing it to myself. At the time I thought I was having a spiritual crisis of some kind but in retrospect, my spirit was trying to break free from the confines I'd put on it and my approach to new experiences. It wasn't until my walk across Spain that I fully came to recognize that for what it was.

Being on someone else's schedule was profoundly prophetic, in retrospect. I was forced to simply be. I could not push the river and change the current when we were broken down on the side of the road, waiting for a plane that was continuously delayed, or conceding to the group's vote to stick to the scheduled shopping trip for souvenirs instead of accepting an offer to meet up with local friends of our tour guide and experiencing something truly once-in-a-lifetime albeit not on the itinerary. It's hard to recognize the beauty of being stuck when you're stuck in it but, in hindsight, it's character defining, and I wouldn't change a single shared memory or experience.

Fifteen years later and I still am in touch with my bunkmate and, by extension, our tour guide. I learned camels are stinky; yaks milk is what you'd expect it to be; Gobi means desert (so the Gobi Desert literally means "desert desert"); Mongolian women are fierce, strong, and liberated; the lake region is truly tranquil, ger tents are warm and homey; music and cultural traditions are treasured; nomadic people are welcoming and warm; and I loved every second of my time there and am thankful for every moment of stuckness I experienced. Mongolia was a teacher in ways I've not experienced since.

Common Scams and (Avoidable) Sticky Situations

The world is full of creative scams. Visitors to your own hometown may even encounter scams that you would never notice as a local "in the know." Natasha's British husband was shocked by the number of scams she encountered in London, as no one had ever bothered to target him, being a local. Scams can vary from overtly obvious to intricate, from easily avoidable to requiring careful attention to avoid. Compiled below is a list of the most common scams you may encounter and what you can do to avoid them.

* **Taxi drivers who pretend their meters are broken to charge excess fees** - Insist on using the meter even if you must find a new driver. If the issue persists or no other drivers are available, agree on a price before you get in the car and be sure to negotiate if culturally appropriate. Try to only use official taxis, Ubers, or driving services—this will be especially important when leaving the airport. And just like at home, where possible, verify your driver is who their profile says they are and that the license plate matches before you get in the car!

* **Offer of a gimmicky photo shot that you are charged for after the fact** - If someone has made the effort of setting up a cheesy photo op for tourists, they are likely not doing it out of the goodness of their hearts and will ask to be paid once you have taken the photo. If someone is being persistent about you taking a photo in specific location (such as in front of the Pyramids or holding their exotic snake (not a euphemism), be sure to politely decline or agree to a price before documenting the occasion.

* **Free items that are never actually free** - If a vendor offers you a free bracelet, flower, or any other good, we assure you they will seek payment for it once it is in your hands. Don't take the bait. This one is tried and true, from the streets of New York City to sidewalks of Paris, and easy to fall for. Just remember, while the majority of the humans you'll meet are genuine and kind, there are still those who are opportunistic. We want you to travel openly (mind and heart) while still fine-tuning your bullshit radar.

* **Free Maps** - Similar to the free items mentioned above, there are scams that involve receiving a free map (or other helpful travel service). To be fair, in these cases they often do actually provide the map, but the person offering will take you to an out of the way location where they receive a finder's fee for bringing you into a "hard sell" environment. You may also then be required to pay to get back to your original location. These often end in more of a waste of time than money, but still ought to be avoided.

* **Free ""shows" and the offer of the '"good stuff in the 'back"** - First, yuck! Stay away from these at all costs. Both these scenarios are commonly followed by either requiring you to pay for an extremely overpriced two-drink minimum or forcing you to buy something expensive from their shop. There have also been stories of the staff not allowing you to leave the premises until you have paid these extortionate costs, even going as far as to involve corrupt police officers. To avoid this always be sure to buy legitimate tickets – if you're unsure how, check with your hostel staff, and NEVER go into the "back room" of any establishment. Stay safe!

* **Colored plastic bags** - Not a scam per se, but in one market Natasha learned that the shop owners gave different colored plastic bags for purchases to people based on their negotiating skills (or lack thereof) as a way of warning other shop owners. While not detrimental, it is simpler to just throw your stuff into your own reusable bag and start fresh with each vendor.

* **Your intended destination is "closed"** - Your taxi driver may tell you your hostel has closed, but he knows a nice hotel nearby. A stranger at the entrance of a temple may tell you it is closed to tourists today for religious services. In both cases the '"helpful 'stranger" may actually be paid a fee to take you to an alternative location when really the original location of your choosing is still very much open.

* **Drug Fines** - Even if drugs are legal or common in a location you are visiting, never take the drugs out of the establishment in which they were provided. In some cases, the drugs are only legal under the license of the establishment and in other cases the staff have paid off local officials to turn a blind eye. In either case, should you take the items out of the establishment, you can potentially be fined, jailed, or blackmailed. We don't mean to scare but assume you're being watched by the local police. There have even been stories of police watching people cross from one bar's legal perimeter into the next, waiting to take advantage of the situation. In short, enjoy your slice of space cake where you purchased it. →

* **Eating in the main tourist square**
  - Perhaps not a scam in the traditional sense, but you will be paying top dollar for often subpar food (and that's a scam in our opinion).
* **Damaged Equipment** - Take photos of any rental equipment so you can't be charged for any damages you did not inflict. We mentioned this in the rental car section. Same applies for everything else!
* **Found gems/jewelry/expensive items**
  A rare and quite old scam but, nevertheless, if anyone says they have an expensive item (that they potentially found, but don't have the time to deal with) that you can buy for cheap and sell elsewhere for more money – get away from that person.
* **Bribes** - We have both been lucky enough to have never found ourselves in the situation of being requested to pay a bribe, or we were potentially naive enough to think it was an official fee. Regardless, in areas where government structures are weak, this may still be possibility. Take some time to do some research and familiarize yourself with the safest option for the locale of your choosing. As we've mentioned before, sometimes it's easier just to pay the fee and go.
* **Theft outside famous monuments**
  - When in famous tourist areas, take extra care of your belongings. Unfortunately pickpockets, drive-by bag snatches, and other clever rouses are still quite common. We have even seen a scenario on the lawn next to the Eiffel Tower where it is popular to drink wine on picnic blankets and people leave their valuables lying next to them. Children will walk by and drop a piece of paper on your blanket; when they lean down to pick it up, they take your valuables with them. Secured zippered bags, travel wallets, and careful attention to your belongings can often provide enough extra security for you to not be worth their time.
* **Public Wi-Fi** - Never access bank accounts or sensitive personal information on public or unsecure Wi-Fi, and be cautious of any free chargers, which may have been tampered with to install malware on your device.

This list is not exhaustive and is not intended to scare you. In discussing this list with other travelers, we found it was common for people to only have lost a few dollars or hours of their time or not even be aware that they had been scammed until years later. However, being aware of these types of scams can help you recognize when to just say "no thank you" and carry on with your day.

Kim

I experienced a similar closed situation during a trip to the Dominican Republic. While walking along the beach near a host of resorts, we came across a beautiful, undeveloped and tourist-free cove. When we reached the end of the resort stretch and went to continue along the people-free section, a police officer emerged from a thicket of trees and informed us this stretch of beach was closed and that we must turn back around and return to our hotel. I watched mystified as beach walker after beach walker was turned away, right where the beach chairs ran out. Having a healthy respect for authority, I obliged the first day and returned to my hotel, then proceeded to bitch to my partner about it the rest of the night. I was determined to explore that cove the next day.

The following day, once again, out pops the officer to tell us that our walk is finished, and we were to turn around. This time I feigned incomprehension and continued past him, through the invisible barrier he'd so securely been guarding. We proceeded to make our way around the barren but beautiful cove. He did not attempt to stop us. My reward for being brave enough to venture forth came in the form of a beautiful Hatian woman emerging from the trees about a mile up the beach. She walked straight up, embraced us both in a friendly hug, and invited us to enjoy a beer at the local beach bar and restaurant owned and run by Mr. Elvis. As we sat, sipping our Presidentes, we spoke with Elvis at length. He informed us that the local authorities are paid off by the hotels to deter tourists from exploring the other side of the cove, essentially trying to put the smaller, local businesses out of service. While Elvis did confirm that if we were to venture much further unaccompanied, we'd likely encounter banditos, the trek from our hotel was quite safe. Every day for the remainder of our trip, we made the three-mile round trip to support Elvis and spend time with the locals, proud of our adventurous spirit, and humbled by their hospitality.

10 Bucket List Ideas

To check off your list

31. Dive with sharks in Cape Town, South Africa .... ☐

32. Hike the South American Andes Mountains .... ☐

33. Crew on a sailboat from Portugal to Greece .... ☐

34. Meet a hundred-year-old tortoise in the Galapagos .... ☐

35. Cross the Drake Passage from Argentina to Antarctica .... ☐

36. Fish off a wharf in Greenland .... ☐

37. Race falcons in the mountains of Kazakhstan .... ☐

38. Ride a camel in the Sahara Desert .... ☐

39. Marvel at the Pyramids in Egypt .... ☐

40. Ride the chocolate and cheese train from Montreux and visit the Gruyère cheese and Nestlé chocolate factories in Switzerland ..... ☐

115

5

BACKPACKERS, FLASHPACKERS & BRATPACKERS

PACKING & (CULTURAL) PERCEPTIONS

Remember, in your travels you'll meet two kinds of tourists—those who pack light and those who wish they had.
—Rick Steves, Packing Smart and Traveling Light

BACKPACKERS (n)

"Backpacking can be described as an independent, often international, low-budget way of travelling...Backpackers generally travel for a longer period of time than most other tourists, and they tend to travel in several different countries during their time away... A backpacker can be on the road from a few weeks to several years." (As We Travel | Travel the World)

FLASHPACKERS (n)

"Not to be confused with a naked backpacker! Flashpackers are usually a little bit older than the standard beer swilling, party hostel staying backpacker. They are similar to their younger selves in that they also have an intrepid ethos of adventure and fun, yet they are likely to have a little extra cash and experience. The extra cash means that flashpackers might sometimes spend a bit more on accommodation in order to avoid the twenty bed dorms or choose a one-hour flight instead of the packed train, followed by a local bus, another local bus, and then a ferry. Or they might splash out on meals in restaurants instead of ramen noodles and white bread in the hostel kitchen." (HuffPost)

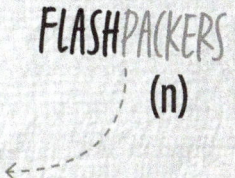

BRATPACKERS (n)

"Now bratpackers are very likely to be eating ramen noodles or $1 rice on a daily basis as their priority is typically drinking buckets of beer or copious amounts of local alcohol, which (let's be honest) could also lead to being a naked backpacker... Think of groups like the large number of partying Australian backpackers acting like larrikans in Bali or the backpackers who treat every night as a Full Moon Party in Thailand. Bratpackers are travelers who have no awareness or respect for local customs or cultures and are more interested in getting ripped than experiencing the country they are in." (HuffPost)

Natasha

Journeying through Laos, I took on a travel buddy. She was beautiful in every sense of the word — sparkling personality with equally shining hair. I quickly noticed she spent hours of our adventure time blow-drying and straightening her hair only to look the same (at least to me) in the end! Over the course of the trip, she began to realize her efforts were completely in vain. The humidity, heat, mud, and rain rendered her products completely useless. She lugged these items from city to city with the excess weight in her pack. It wasn't until later in the trip when we found ourselves in the middle of a freak storm in Luang Prabang that I learned of the hours of drunken entertainment and appreciation that a blow-dryer could provide.

Basically, we were a little bit drunk (perhaps a lot), made a fort out of the blankets, and turned on all the blow-dryers we could find to create a makeshift heater. Then we used a blow-dryer to melt the cheese on a frozen 7-Eleven personal pizza. Come to think of it, we may have been really stoned as well. Either way, it was the hardest I had ever laughed in my life, so a little blow-dryer may not be the worst thing in the world to have in your bag (but only if you plan to use it for pizza).

We'll unpack a lot of topics in this chapter, but let's start with packing. Rick Steves is a true master when it comes to packing for travel. Not a vacation. Travel! His philosophy is to pack smart and travel light because "You can't travel heavy, happy, and cheap. Pick two." The goal is to get down to one pack. Singular. There's no added value or freedom by having one backpack fully loaded on your back and another day pack on your front. We've been there, tried that, and ultimately chucked the added weight; you just don't need that much stuff. Multiples aren't encouraged, except underwear, and you really can go without those too. While it might seem daunting to get everything for your trip into one pack, the truth is, with a couple smart layering pieces and a few well-considered versatile clothing choices, you'll be ready for any situation you may find yourself in. Trust us.

Regarding your pack size, you don't need to travel with a giant pack. Ideally you won't have to check your bag (ever) unless you want to. We all know someone who's lost their luggage, ourselves included. It's a pain in the ass and completely avoidable. By having a pack small enough to fit in a standard overhead compartment (larger than a school backpack but smaller than a large suitcase—think between 40 and 60 liters), you'll have an easy time clearing customs and walking out the front door of your new destination instead of wasting precious time waiting in a baggage claim. There's a ton of options out there. We suggest visiting your local camp or travel store and testing out a few different sizes, but we both agree a 65 L bag is more than sufficient. If you're struggling to make it all fit, look for a backpack with a detachable day pack. Another option is to pack a day pack (think an old school backpack) that actually folds and packs into itself like a little burrito. This can tuck into a pack pocket or lay inside until you want it for a city excursion or day trip. Just remember, anything you purchase or carry will eventually need to come out or be packed into your main pack when you fold up and pack away your day pack for its next use.

It is entirely possible to pack the same stuff for one week or one month, but it's always important to consider the climate of where you'll be traveling. If you're traveling for six months, a year, or even longer, consider swapping out seasonal items at a local consignment or thrift shop. This is a cost-effective way to change up your wardrobe while keeping your pack light and staying on budget. By keeping items like makeup, hair care products, perfumes, and lotions to a minimum, you free yourself from the burden of added weight. →

Your pack may feel light while you're still at home making your final packing list, but it becomes a whole different kind of heavy when your hostel is seventeen blocks from the train station.

We cannot emphasize this enough: stick to packing basics. You don't need to be the Instagram-ready flashpacker, clogging up their pack with unnecessary weight that, in truth, they really don't need. You'll be sexier and more alluring dancing in your hiking boots than any local in the club! Remember, you're the exotic foreign traveler now, and this new identity goes a long way toward striking up conversations, receiving invitations, and dancing the night away!

You're beautiful. Woman. Man. Nonbinary. Trans. Gay. Lesbian. Bisexual. Queer. Leave your armor at home and let the world meet you!

Those that care don't matter and those that matter don't care. The travelers you'll meet that matter and leave an imprint on your heart will love you without any added bells and whistles. Trust us. Less really is more.

Toiletries, Hair Appliances & Electronics
You Should Consider Leaving Home

Items you should consider leaving home include (gasp) most makeup and hair products. Certain makeup creates a liquids nightmare in airports, not to mention the risk of bottles leaking or spilling in your pack. If they're more than the standard three ounce travel size, you'll have to check your bag instead of bringing it as a carry on, risking a lost luggage situation. Additionally, not all hostels have mirrors in the dorms, therefore bratpackers end up jamming up bathrooms with their primping and preening. Consider tinted sunscreen as a sun-safe, glowing, dewy alternative. Remember, stay nimble. If you must travel with some sparkles, keep them within carry-on standards.

For hair products, again opt for travel sizes or all-in-one options like Dr. Bronner's liquid or bar soap. This amazing product served us both well while walking the Camino de Santiago as a shampoo, body wash, detergent, and a toothpaste alternative (so long as you get the mint version). If you're using refillable travel-size toiletry bottles, opt for silicone where you can eek out every last ounce of gooey goodness.

Leave hair dryers, flat irons, and electric toothbrushes at home. Not only are they heavy and unnecessary, but they'll require specific voltage where, if you don't have the proper adapter, they may end up shorting a fuse or, worse, starting a fire where you're staying. Depending on where you're staying, your accommodation may have a hair appliance for you to borrow.

For what it's worth, we believe you're beautiful, bedhead and all!

A note on hygiene

While the free-living bohemian persona looks attractive in the movies, if you don't wash yourself or your hair frequently, it leaves a gross film on headrests in trains, planes, and on hostel pillowcases. Be mindful of your hygiene; just because you may be traveling alone, that doesn't mean you're not sharing spaces with others. All we're suggesting is mindful consideration without all the froufrou.

Kim

When I reread journal entries from all my travels, not once do I lament or mourn the loss of my makeup, blow-dryer, or high heels. I mostly wore hiking boots and flip-flops, even if I had on a dress or a blousy top. I ate out at restaurants, drank in a lot pubs, danced in a lot of discos, had a lot of crushes, and entertained many dates (well, the backpacker version of dating) throughout my years of traveling. By no means was I a stunning beauty, but my confidence in traveling alone and my I-don't-give-a-shit attitude while dancing in my hiking boots made me vibrant, approachable, and allowed me to connect with the people I was meeting (locals and travelers alike) on a level beneath the surface of beauty. Truthfully, I've never felt more beautiful than when I'm feeling confident, and I've never felt more confident than when out exploring this world.

Most electronics and adapters are truly unnecessary. We were both fortunate to travel at a time when unplugging from the Matrix was still an easy option. It didn't hurt that US cell phone plans were not as competitive with international pricing or package options as they are today, making it cost prohibitive to travel with a phone at the time. Additionally, payphones (do these still exist?) with country specific calling cards and internet cafes made it easy to connect with family and friends back home while fully being present in whatever part of the world we were individually in.

As payphones disappear by way of the dodo and Google Maps discerns our location with greater accuracy, the need for a digital detox to intentionally become physically and emotionally lost in a foreign land is becoming harder to articulate to first-time travelers. For this reason, we ask you to take a moment to reflect on which devices you think you need and which you know you'll want. Then pick one that will serve all your purposes and try to remember to pack it away so you can become properly lost wherever you presently are.

We feel leaving your phone or electronic devices at home greatly reduces the need to check out what's happening in the virtual landscape back home and instead check in to the events presently taking shape around you. That said, many countries are well connected to Wi-Fi, so bringing your phone and leaving it in airplane mode can serve as an inexpensive way to stay connected without overburdening yourself with multiple heavy electronics to manage.

If what we've outlined isn't enough to have you pair down to one device over many, consider these final points:

* **They're heavy** - remember, every ounce counts
* **They're expensive** - and a pain in the ass to replace

As a traveler, you have enough to worry about just keeping track of your passport and cash without having to worry about having a highly sought-after electronic device getting lost or stolen.

Assuming you're not going completely off the grid, you'll be bringing at least one adapter depending on how many countries you plan to visit. There are multipronged adapters that work in multiple countries but can be bulkier to stow. It is possible to risk shorting out both your appliance and tripping the breaker at your accommodation if your device is not aligned with the proper voltage. Be sure to research, before you leave home, the proper shape and voltage adapter for the countries you plan on visiting. Electronic gadgets have come a long way and are more compact and interchangeable than they once were. Inquire with your host or hostel as they may even have voltage-specific appliances for you to borrow or rent for a small charge. Your electronic device can actually catch fire if the voltage is incorrect! ➔

Natasha

I once set my blow-dryer on fire trying to use it with a simple plug-in adapter. I am still in thankful disbelief that my entire head of hair didn't go up in flames along with it. A lesson I do not want you to learn the hard way!

Lastly, we understand you're going to eventually get bored; between extended waits in airports, overnight train rides, and those rest days where you're just hungover, exhausted, or need to chill out. We acknowledge the instant gratification your electronic device can provide. Consider instead bringing a paperback book from home to read in your down time. Make sure it's a book you're comfortable leaving or losing somewhere. We've harped on weight enough, so save your hardbound copy of War and Peace for another time. Some might argue that by packing your e-reader you're saving space with e-books or Audible (we love both), however, by traveling with an actual book, you open yourself up to a literary world of options. Let us explain.

Many hostels and even cafes have an entertainment nook within their common room spaces that contain things like board games and books. Furthermore, most advertise a leave a book, take a book philosophy. For example, if you don't have a book, you can borrow one to read during your visit. If you have a book that you've finished reading, you can simply swap yours out for another one before you leave. Not only are you adding to the ever-changing landscape of literary options for future backpackers, but you're also not tapping into your travel budget to replace the book you've finished. At the end of the day, if you're really not keen on packing, unpacking, and repacking said book, you can simply leave it for the next traveler to enjoy—unlike your iPad, Kindle, or Nook.

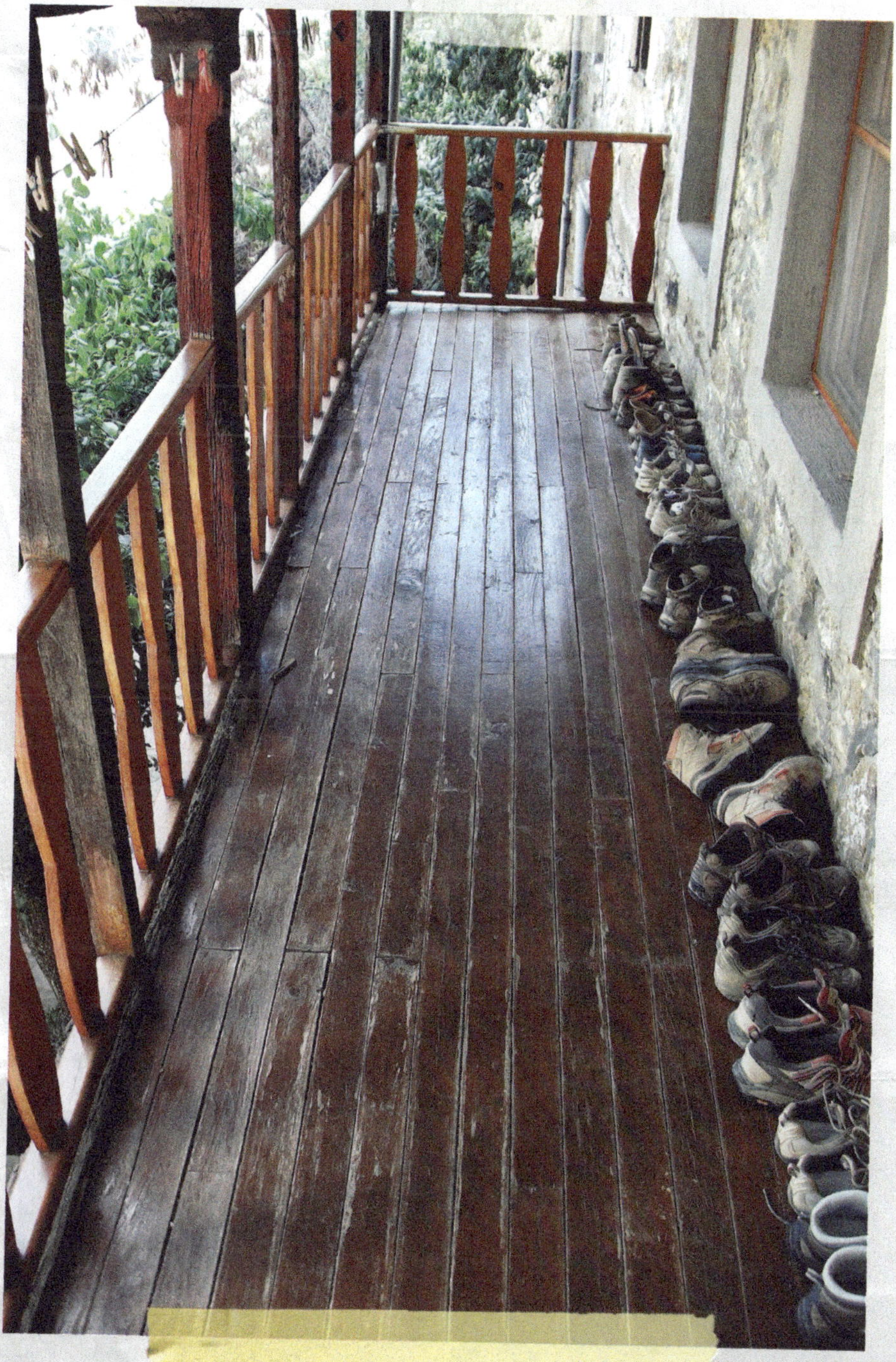

Packing Suggestions & Considerations

Everything should be able to serve more than one purpose. For example, you don't need to pack pajamas when you can sleep in your leggings and then wear them out to explore the city the next day.

The Essentials

- **Large backpack:**
  We recommend 40 L to 65 L packs for most men and women, with or without detachable day pack.
- **Money belt or travel belt:**
  To safely store passport, money, credit cards, transportation tickets/passes, and emergency medical documentation.
- **Small hotel sewing kit:**
  Good for digging out splinters or patching up the hole you tore in your jeans playing Frisbee.
- **Medical kit:**
  In a resealable bag, include adhesive bandages (plasters), antibacterial ointment, ibuprofen, loperamide, an antihistamine, and a couple safety pins.

- **Menstruation** supplies and contraceptives (see page 128).

- Travel journal and something to write with.

Versatile Basics

- Leggings—1-2 pairs (can be dressed up, dressed down, or slept in)

- Shorts—1 pair

- Skirt or athletic skort (optional)—1 pair

- Maxi dress

- Convertible hiking pants (that zip off into shorts)—1 pair

- Fast-drying or wicking T-shirts—2-3

- Long sleeve T-shirt—1-2 for layering

- Wrinkle-resistant "going out" top–1-2 but you'll probably find yourself not getting as dressed up as you did at home............ ☐

- Packable down jacket–a lightweight, packable version will serve you well not only in colder climates but also in frigid air conditioning (bonus: it can double as a pillow on long train or bus rides)............ ☐

- Rain jacket–packable............ ☐

- Fleece jacket (optional) – for layering............ ☐

- Sarong or wide scarf – for head or shoulder covering when visiting certain countries or religious monuments. This can also serve as a beach towel or blanket given the circumstances............ ☐

- Trail shoes – select a pair of lightweight trail running sneakers that can get you up most mountains and walk comfortably around a city for hours. If you're planning a mountain expedition, then you'll want hiking boots, otherwise solid trail sneakers are just fine............ ☐

- Sandals or flip-flops (thongs) – backpackers love their Chacos: you can wade through a river, hike a mountain, and still wear them with a dress, but if they're not for you (we're team Teva, all the way), think in terms of a versatile sandal that you can wear with a dress or wade through water in............ ☐

- Board shorts or bathing suit – or just wear your underwear............ ☐

- Sports bra – 2 versatile ones can serve multiple functions and are more comfortable and easier to pack and care for than underwire ones............ ☐

- Underwear – this one's up to you, but if you're traveling for a long time, you'll probably replace them along the way; going commando is always an option – just saying............ ☐

- Micro-fiber towel (small)............ ☐

Natasha

A few minutes of extra preparation is always a good idea. When traveling in South Africa, I was invited along with a few others on a 5-kilometer jog through a nearby national park. As a fairly athletic person only going a few miles, I threw on my running shoes, drank a glass of water, and ran out the door. As the jog commenced a local friend outlined the simple turns of the trail so we could all meet at the end. As everyone ran at different paces, the group slowly split up. Another gentleman and I casually chatted as we ran through the gorgeous landscape. As time passed, we expected to find the group waiting around every corner. Slowly we began to realize that we had taken the wrong trail. We continued, expecting the well-marked path to eventually loop back to the start. As the hours passed, we realized that every turn of the trail began to look the same. We had no water, no food, no sunscreen, no bug spray, no phone, and no knowledge of how to get back. Unbeknownst to us at the time, our friends simultaneously spent hours running the trails looking for us and assuming the worst. Fast forward fourteen hours and 35 kilometers to the rescue team finding us—dehydrated, sun burnt, hungry, bug-bitten, and with generally bruised spirits. After tending to our needs, we received a stern lecture about our preparedness. The lesson I learned the hard way is to always be sure to have a few basics (water, snack, phone) with you in any unfamiliar area even if you think it's just a quick outing.

Menstruation
Traveling on Your Period

Cassandra Brooklyn confidently shares how to have a bloody good time no matter where you are in the world in an online article in World Nomads. As she puts it, go with what you know, and we agree. However, as always, you should be prepared for the unexpected.

In most countries, you're likely to find some form of menstrual hygiene product at either a grocery store or local bodega, but keep in mind, they may not always be as readily available or exactly the products you're used to using. On that note, it's worth remembering that toilet paper and running water may not always be available in what passes as a bathroom in some parts of the world. So where does that leave us?

Disclaimer! We are not doctors and the information below should not be taken as medical advice. We have, however, had quite a few periods while traveling over the years.

We have provided some practical guidance below.

- ★ Pads are by far the most common hygiene product on the world market. As an example, it's quite common for tampons in China to be on the very top shelves to appeal to foreign women. At the time of this writing, roughly 2% of Chinese women use tampons.
- ★ Take a backup of your preferred hygiene method along in your pack—including wipes. We know this takes up valuable space, but just trust us on this one.

- ★ If it's tampons or bust, we highly recommend ensuring you are comfortable using a standard cotton tampon without an applicator, as this type is far more common across the world. They are readily available in US stores wherever tampons are sold.
- ★ Be mentally prepared to use whatever method is locally available. Sometimes no matter what you prefer or what you pack along, the unexpected occurs.

If you're considering changing period tactics, be sure to give any new product you're considering a test run at home before you travel abroad. Alternatives to tampons and pads include reusable options such as menstruation cups, cloth pads, and period panties (designed to absorb your flow, then you wash and rewear). If you're keen on a particular brand and will only be traveling for a short period of time, then we recommend packing a stash in your pack Also, leave the box at home. Put the tampons or pads in a resealable bag or stuff them in all the empty spaces of your pack. If, however, you're planning to let the wind's direction guide your international itinerary, it might be worth exploring reusable menstruation cups. This way, if you find yourself camping or in a remote or rural region, you can confidently stem your flow.

> **PRO-TIP**
>
> If you're the type of gal whose Aunt Flo visits every month like clockwork, it might be a huge shock if your cycle pops off the rails when you're traveling. Stress, flying, changing time zones, even changes to your eating habits can all impact the timeliness of your cycle while traveling. Take these delays in stride and know you're not alone. If you haven't had unprotected sex recently, then you're probably just fine and stressing out about being late will only compound the delay.

Natasha

Navigating my period abroad was a lesson I learned time and time again. Every time I thought I had it down to a science, another curve ball was thrown my way. Like many women in the US, I learned to manage my time of the month by using a lovely (albeit terrible for the environment) smooth plastic applicator. Little did I know, despite bleeding women living in every corner of the world, that this product is not sold in the majority of countries found on this little planet of ours. Not to mention that in plenty of countries discussion of such unseemly topics can be met with varying levels of taboo or can even outright prohibit you from entering certain premises. Please accept my next few situational experiences with a pinch of salt—times may have changed in some places, both culturally and economically, from my last visit, or my experiences may have been unique to the region, subgroup, or even the people I encountered.

Australia

Arriving after a forty-hour flight (the cheapest one I could find but with an absurd number of layovers) was an exhausting experience—long customs lines were only made more unbearable by worsening cramps and a looming period. On the way to my accommodation, I stopped at a local pharmacy to pick up some tampons. Let me tell you that after a forty-hour flight may be one of the worst times to learn to use an applicator-free tampon for the first time. Please heed my warning and practice in advance.

Hong Kong/Macau

Wandering the aisles of period pads in desperate search for a tampon was not how I expected to spend a few hours after an evening in what can only be described as the "Las Vegas of the East." It doesn't matter how much a place looks like home (if your home is Las Vegas), with state-of-the-art casinos and looming hotels plastered with common Western brands, local culture is local culture and supply and demand is king. And there was no demand for tampons.

Indonesia

After months spent searching for tampons in a haystack of pads throughout Asia, I was pleasantly surprised to find them readily available in Bali thanks in part to the influx of Western tourists throughout the past decade. What I wasn't pleasantly surprised to find was the exorbitant cost of them. On average, the cost of tampons was approximately five to eight times more expensive than pads.

Laos

By the time I arrived, I was prepared that the less trodden paths of Laos were not going to have my preferred hygiene method. By that point I was an experienced traveler and felt well prepared for the unknown—I had toilet paper and tampons ready to go. What I did not anticipate was being on a "slow boat" for the better part of two full days with nothing but a squat toilet available and no running water. After ruining a lesser loved T-shirt and emptying a bottle of water to clean my hands after using an applicator-free tampon over a sloshing squat toilet on a moving boat (apologies for the graphics), I would have given anything to have in my possession a pair of period panties and a surplus of hand sanitizing wipes!

Zambia

By the time I arrived in Zambia, I thought I had experienced it all (familiar right?)—dirty toilets, squat toilets, no toilet paper, no running water, etc.... I was ready for whatever life was going to throw at me. It was a full day bus journey that stopped me in my tracks. In my experience, traveling by bus in other regions of the world usually included a rest stop every six hours or so that included a bathroom and snack counter of some kind, and so I assumed this journey would be the same. Imagine my surprise when the bus came to no such stops. The bus ended up pulling over on the side of a field where all the men got out and went to one side of the bus to relieve themselves, and all the women together walked a slightly longer distance, into the high grass for added privacy, to do the same. In that moment, I also noticed that all the women wore traditional wrap skirts that were easy to lift up to knee height while squatting down in the moderate privacy of their fabrics and high grass. I just stood there dumbfounded in my trousers, desperate to relieve myself, and unable to do so without completely exposing myself to an entire busload of men. A local woman sensed my desperation and came over with an extra cloth to shield me for a few moments. I can only thank my lucky stars that I was not on my period that day. However, in case you ever find yourself in such situations, remember "the power of the shawl" and always carry one with you. Equally, I urge you to have multiple hygiene methods readily available—period undies or longer-wearing menstruation cups might be just what you need on such an occasion.

A final note, in many Asian countries (and potentially other regions) women are actually banned from entering religious temples while on their period. We have never personally come across any request for verification, but remember to be respectful of local customs and use your best judgment. For more on this, check out the following online article: Feminine Hygiene Around The World.

Birth Control

Kim

Finding a birth control option for when I was traveling months at a time proved frustrating and challenging throughout my twenties. For years I struggled to find an option that best suited my lifestyle and properly regulated my hormones. Like others, I am not a fan of taking pills, so the pill was never an option for me. At the time innovations in contraception were beginning to come to the market, and I was happy to try them all to find a fit. For a while I was on the patch but didn't like that you had to wear it in different locations on your body each month or how the edges rolled and picked up fibers from my clothing. I tried the shot but couldn't get past having my period every single day for the better part of three months, so I was not keen to keep shooting. I mean, isn't one of the perks of birth control eventually not getting a (heavy) period? Eventually I found my way to the ring, which I remained on for many years. When it first came to market, doctors were quite generous in handing out additional samples that I would save for my next adventure abroad. Eventually though, I couldn't gain access to more than one prescription ring at a time, which left me precariously unprotected during several of my overseas adventures. Not only did this impact the irregularity of my hormones, but it added a lot of mental stress to sexual situations. At the time, IUDs were not as readily available, and there are still doctors in the US to this day who advise against inserting an IUD in any woman who has not (yet) had children, regardless of age and circumstance. News flash, not every woman will have a child; I never did. Had I been a stronger advocate for myself at the time, I would have insisted on an IUD and saved myself a lot of stress.

PRO-TIP

Whatever your preferred method of birth control, condoms are always a great backup to be sure "you're covered" and protected against STIs.

Condom Sense

Whether or not you choose to use birth control, if you decide to have sex while traveling, you absolutely must have and use condoms. Do not expect the other person to supply them. Be in charge of your own sexual health, at home and abroad! Our advice, bring your own preferred brand since the availability and quality of condoms can vary by region. Trust us, it's always better to have a few stashed away in your purse or day pack, just in case you meet the love of your life drunk at a bar—or simply encounter a beautiful stranger with a lovely accent.

The Pill

If the pill is your tried and true, be sure to request a few extra packs from the doc before you go, just keep in mind that the change in time zone could impact the time of your next dose. If your insurance won't cover more than a one-month supply at a time, check out your local Planned Parenthood or Health Department to see if they can offer a multimonth solution. If you find your trip extended or lose a pack, a replacement option may be available at a local pharmacy, even while traveling through off the beaten path locales. The Global Oral Contraceptive Availability website is a great resource as well.

The Ring & Patch

With either option, if your current insurance or doctor will permit it, request an extra month's prescription or two, explaining that you will be traveling for an extended period of time, possibly to remote areas where a local pharmacy may not be within easy access. With the ring, the pharmacist will probably tell you to keep it refrigerated and that is definitely best practice. However, a friendly internet search has informed us that you can leave it at room temperature for up to four months if you keep it out of direct sunlight. Do keep in mind that your bag may often be exposed to the elements while on the road. Depending on where you adventure, it's not uncommon that your backpack may travel on top of the bus you're riding, in over one-hundred-degree heat, for hours at a time. So be sure to speak to your doctor, research the climate for your desired destination, and use your best judgment.

Implant, IUD & Shot

While we do not recommend starting one of these treatments within a few days or weeks of your first trip abroad, if you've already been on them a while and are comfortable with how your body is responding, then the sky is the limit! Not only can these methods last for months to years at a time, they are brilliant and easy options for living that travel life on the road. Be sure to confirm your next injection appointment or replacement date and schedule it well in advance of your trip. Again, it's best to be sure you and your body are comfortable on any of these methods for a few months before hitting the road.

Sponge, Diaphragm & Cervical Cap

While neither of us have any experience with these, sources say to keep them out of direct sunlight, always be sure to pack a spare in case of loss or damage, and don't forget the spermicide!

Family Planning Method

We can't, in good consciousness, recommend this approach to birth control while traveling, even for individuals embarking on their journey with committed partners. This is not to speak against the commitment of your partnership, but rather to indicate the amount of additional stress you will be putting on your body while traveling. The amount your natural biorhythm and cycle can fluctuate from the chaos of changing time zones, diet changes, stress, lack of sleep, and sheer excitement could lead to miscalculating the timing of your cycle and result in an unplanned pregnancy.

For a more detailed overview of available options, with some excellent advice to women wishing to remain on birth control while traveling, seek out Ashley Canino's online article "Safe Travels: Birth control for when you're abroad" where she outlines with great care options and resources for staying protected while traveling abroad.

Whichever method you choose, choose what's right for you.

10
Bucket List Ideas
To check off your list

41. Enjoy a savory breakfast in Kyoto, Japan ☐
42. Drink absinthe in Prague ☐
43. Eat reindeer jerky in Malmö, Switzerland ☐
44. Visit the Onion Market in Bern, Switzerland ☐
45. Teach English in Seoul or rural South Korea ☐
46. Explore Spain's Sherry Triangle ☐
47. Visit the island of Malta ☐
48. Stay up all night in Ibiza ☐
49. Soak in the Blue Lagoon, Iceland ☐
50. Eat with your hands in Ethiopia ☐

137

6

WHERE TO REST YOUR WEARY HEAD—

BUNK BEDS, COUCH SURFING, CAMPING &....

To awaken quite alone in a strange town is one of the pleasantest sensations in the world. You are surrounded by adventure.
—Freya Stark, Baghdad Sketches

A Solo Backpacker's Accommodations Cheat Sheet

Want to make friends and go out with people from all over the world? Then <u>hostels</u> are for you!

Looking to immerse yourself in the culture and spend your time like a local? <u>Homestays</u> and <u>couch surfing</u> might be just what you're looking for.

Do you appreciate quiet solitude, have a healthy travel budget and want to spend more time in one location? Check out local offerings from <u>Airbnb and Vrbo</u>.

ARE YOU THE WILDERNESS TYPE? WANT A MORE RUSTIC EXPERIENCE IN THE GREAT OUTDOORS? <u>CAMPING</u> MIGHT SCRATCH THAT ITCH (JUST BE SURE TO BRING BUG SPRAY)!

None of these options are currently available? <u>Hotels</u> to the rescue!

We LOVE (Youth) Hostels

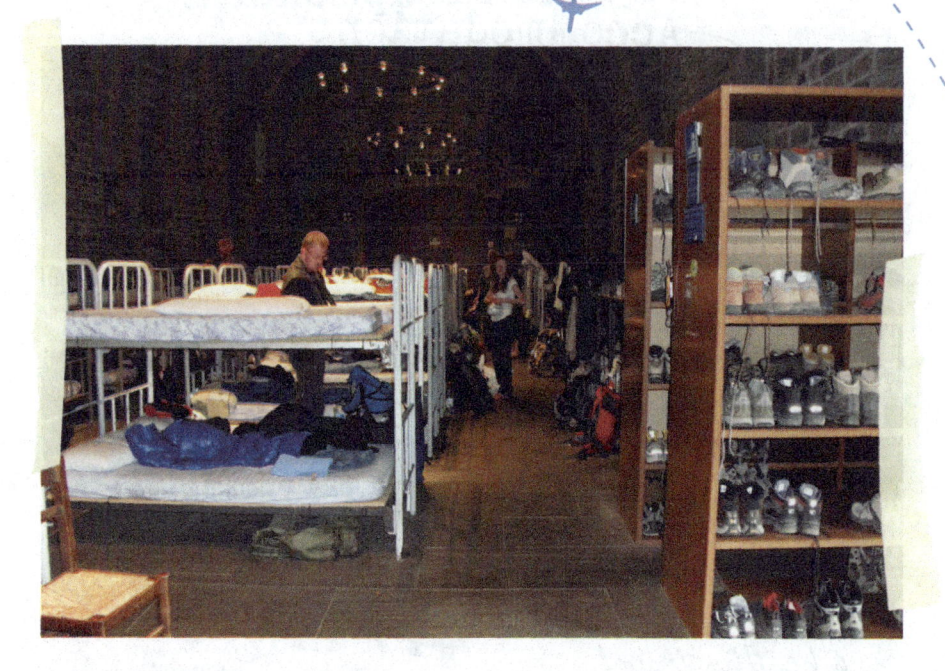

Get comfortable, we're going to spend a lot of time selling you on the benefits of sleeping (and partying) in hostels. In today's era of Airbnb and low-cost luxury lodging, it may seem unnecessary to consider experiencing the novelty of the amenity-modest and sometimes sleep-depriving youth hostel.

There is something uniquely character defining within the backpacking community that develops when you arrive in a strange new place, claim your assigned bunk, secure your valuables, and commune (or commiserate) with the other like-minded, soul searching, vagabonding world citizens assigned to your room. If you're one of the many Americans who have watched the horror movie by the same name and now fear that all hostels are minefields for murder, it's time to let that shitake take go. Just as no person, city, or country are exactly alike, so too are no two youth hostels alike.

With just about all hostels you'll find a full size kitchen with fridge to encourage travelers from all nationalities to cook and share a meal together (more on that later); options for a single, shared, or dorm-style room accommodations (think bunk beds); laundry (this could be coin/card operated); private or shared bathrooms; and usually Wi-Fi or a computer station to let everyone back home know you're safe and sound (computer stations sometimes require dropping coins in a meter every ten minutes or so).

If you have the financial flexibility or can be creative with your budget, there's value in trying to book a private room once a week to ensure at least one solid night of sleep and recovery during your travels. Trust us when we say you expend a lot of energy traveling, meeting new friends, and going out to pubs; and while hostels are fun and affordable, you're not always guaranteed a restful night of sleep in a shared room. It took us many, many years to adhere to this advice because, let's face it, there is always something going on, something to do, and new people to meet along the way and frankly, FOMO is real! Besides, you can sleep when you get home.

PRO-TIP

Some hostels offer same-sex dorm options upon request, such as female-only rooms for those less comfortable with mixed-gender sleeping. Dorms can range in capacity from two, four, eight, twelve, eighteen, or even a staggering hundred-person room in Roncevalles, Spain.

More Reasons We Prefer Hostels

Being single women traveling alone in our twenties and early thirties, we honed a heightened level of intuition and instinct. This was further fine-tuned because of staying in hostels and gaining tips and insights from other travelers. Hostels provide a safe and comfortable alternative to hotels for many reasons. The most important (we feel) are highlighted on the following pages.

They're Fun!

Below are just a few of the many benefits and activities you may find yourself enjoying and engaging in while in some corner of this world, should you decide to stay in a youth hostel.

- Pub crawls, trivia nights, walking tours, and other activities to make friends and experience the city!
- Impromptu jam or story sessions—it's not uncommon to meet a traveler carrying a guitar, bongo, or other musical instrument. Some hostels have a bar where you can share stories with other travelers passing through and gather ideas of where to travel next.
- Diversity and community! You will meet the most amazing people in hostels! While, admittedly, not everyone travels as well or as respectfully as others, more often than not you'll connect with someone at every hostel you stay in.
- Travel buddies! Sometimes you meet people you're not ready to say goodbye to.

Many unplanned adventures have happened because of a shared room or pint of beer at a hostel. Remember, you only need to be eighteen years old to drink in many foreign countries!

Natasha

Once while exploring the Cinque Terre I found a village hostel nestled in the mountains that offered bus transportation to the cliffside every hour until 9:00 p.m. I was completely immersed in the cliffside experiences: soaking in the sunset, cliff jumping, and drinking cheap and delicious Italian wine with new friends. By the time the last bus was departing back to my village, I simply wasn't ready to end my night. Sensing my frustration, one of the other backpackers mentioned their guesthouse was just a few minutes' walk away and that there were plenty of beds available. They assured me Mama (the host) would gladly give me a bed for the night. Thrilled by this turn of events, I partied on the cliffs through the night and awoke the next morning for a fresh dip in the Mediterranean before hopping back on the bus to return to my hostel.

Upon arriving back at the hostel I'd previously paid for but never returned to, I was greeted by several emotions and realizations. It turned out the hostel staff had been alerted to my absence and had contacted local authorities, concerned that I may have been kidnapped, injured, or was just generally missing. Apparently, the hostel staff, guests, and Italian police had been looking for me all night.

I had mixed feelings about this realization. At first, I was surprised and confused; I mean, it's just a hostel, and I can decide to stay out all night if I choose to. Next, I was annoyed because they aren't my parents and what I do is of no concern to them. Finally, I was appreciative, because the hostel was located down a dark and windy road through the Italian mountains. Had I fallen ill, been taken, or became lost in the woods, it was nice to know that there were people who actively noticed and would do what they could to find and help me.

The moral of the story is that a hostel can easily become a home away from home, and with that comes extended family who worry about you. While every hostel is different, a good rule of thumb is if you know you are going to stay out all night, just call and give the staff a heads up. Unlike your parents, they will be thrilled that you are out having the time of your life till the sun comes up over the horizon.

They're Safe

All hostels are unique! They really are an expression of the owners, location, and crowds they attract. When you check into a hostel, your bed is noted and accounted for, and someone will notice if you do not return or go missing. In a hostel, you're in a room with other (solo) travelers and that in itself is a comfort in the middle of the night, assuming you didn't book a private room. Some hostels have evening curfews with added security features such as a provided key fob, door code, or an overnight employee monitoring entrances to keep you and others safe. Remember, you're staying with like-minded individuals, and backpackers look out for one another. At least the good ones do. Be a good one!

They're Affordable

Hostels are budget friendly and can afford you the opportunity to explore more and spend less. Shared accommodations can cost anything from a suggested donation to about US$40 per night and usually will land somewhere in between. Costs will range based on proximity to transportation hubs, attractions, and (peak travel) time of year and can also be influenced by physical remoteness, competitive lodging options, and the country you're in. In some cases, this can drive the price higher than the average. Supply and demand are a real thing.

Most have a kitchen, and others may even have a restaurant, food/smoothie service bar, or small convenience shop where you can pick up staple items. These are cheaper than eating out and when you combine your ingredients with a fellow backpacker and cook together, you can pick up some cultural culinary skills too!

Discounts and deals are available for travelers of all ages and will depend on the specific hostels you wish to book. As we mentioned in chapter one, most available discounts are for travelers aged twenty-six or younger, however these may extend to forty years old depending on the individual business. A quick online search for international hostel travel cards, discounts, or youth affiliated deals will net many reputable resources. Many hostels are centrally located relative to everything you're looking to explore. Though not all in the city center, hostels tend to be close to the action and easier to reach via public transportation.

Booking a Hostel

Booking a hostel is super easy, so we're not going to spend a lot of time on the topic. Just about every hostel is on one of the main hostel booking websites or in your guidebook. In the rare event you're traveling to a more remote area where cell service, Wi-Fi, or internet are a bit spottier, a good old-fashioned phone call or walk-in request can usually result in a bed or referral to a nearby alternative with availability. This is really when your Lonely Planet, Fodor's, or Rick Steves guidebooks come in handy, but for the most up-to-date information, sites such as Hostelworld.com or HiHostels.com are excellent alternatives. Finally, it's always best to book or inquire directly with the hostel and not through a third party.

Assuming you haven't planned and accounted for every moment of your international adventure, it's worth leaving space in your itinerary for the unexpected (accommodations) detour. Detours are good and are encouraged! At the end of every day, it will always work out and you'll have a place to sleep.

✈ PRO-TIP

High/Peak (travel) seasons matter, and you might have to reach out to several hostels before you book a bed, so plan accordingly. It may seem tempting to prebook all your hostels in advance of arriving at your destination, but we're here to encourage you to not do this (unless you are going to Munich for Oktoberfest—then please book ahead). At least not for the entire time you're traveling. Too many unforeseen factors can impact your timetable and it would be devastating to lose precious funds that would otherwise keep you on the road longer. Feel confident in prebooking your first night as this will make completing your customs form easier upon entry into a new country, but after that, let the wind carry you where it will.

- **ROOM/HABITACIÓN:** 39
- **BED/CAMA:** 2 LOWER / 2 UPPER
- **WIFI:** haveaniceday

Breakfast / *Desayuno: 7:30 to 10:30 am*
Check out : *12 pm*

A suggestion, visit our **Rooftop bar**, the best place to end the day.

Una sugerencia, visita nuestro **Rooftop Bar**, es el sitio perfecto para acabar el día.

THE HAT

Lock Outs & Bed Assignments

One thing you'll come to discover is most hostels have a period of lock out. This is when all guests—regardless of if it's a rainy day, you're feeling lazy, or you're staying multiple nights—must leave the premises for about three hours. During these hours, hostel staff (or volunteers) strip and wash bedding and clean kitchens, bathrooms, showers, and common rooms. Lock out times are usually explained upon check-in and written on your check-in card/ticket, which also indicates the room, bed, and/or locker number assigned to you.

Hostel Age Restrictions

While most public hostels don't have age restrictions, some do. Age restrictions can indicate both a minimum age limit (typically eighteen years and older, but some may permit younger occupants with guardian approval) and in some cases a maximum age admitted. This is, in part, to allow for younger travelers to feel more comfortable and safer. Finally, while some hostels may allow for traveling families, not all hostel environments are appropriate for younger children. Below are some types of hostels you may come across.

* Membership-based Hostels—brands such as HI (Hosteling International), YHA (Youth Hostel Association of Australia), IHL (Israel Hostels), JHI-Japan (Japan Hostel Group), or CYHA (Croatian Youth Hostel Association) are a great consideration if this is your first time backpacking alone, you plan to be gone more than a few weeks, or if you're still a little nervous about hostels. For a small fee, you gain access to members-only locations (which can be a great advantage if traveling during high season when municipal, public and private hostels may fill up quickly). The hostels are often situated in prime locations. Additional advantages can include reduced tour prices, specials for museums or events, and sometimes even food and drink discounts. While they can sometimes have stricter curfew restrictions, they are very safe and often cater to youth, age twenty-seven or younger.

* Private Hostels—Can cost a bit more but typically do not have age restrictions and, due to the slightly higher price point, can often deter younger or more budget conscience travelers, thereby making them a bit more subdued when it comes to late-night partying, which is great if you're in need of an uninterrupted night of sleep or find yourself traveling a little later in life.

* Municipal Hostels—These are country run or managed. Regions such as northern Spain have a lot of these available to pilgrims journeying on the Camino de Santiago. These are generally open to all and may be altogether free or simply donation based.

Be sure to check the hostel's policies prior to booking to be sure you are admitted upon arrival. Rest assured, whatever age you are, there is always a hostel option to suit you!

Hostel Etiquette & Other Sleeping Considerations

On the road, hostels can become your home away from home: a place to relax, cook, hang with friends, and generally let loose. This said, it's important to remember that while it may feel like home, there are some important etiquette and guidelines for harmonious shared living. The most important thing is to be clean and tidy!

Bedbugs

While we have been lucky enough not to encounter these nasty biters personally, we have met many fellow travelers who have fallen victim to bedbug attacks. To ensure this doesn't happen to you, read hostel reviews and be sure to inspect the seams of your mattress upon check-in. Many, though not all, city hostels discourage using your personal bedding and will require you to rent sheet sets to mitigate the spread of bedbugs. These are stripped and washed daily during lock out.

PRO-TIP

Because peak season requires high bed turnover, this is an easy opportunity to volunteer your cleaning services in exchange for a free night's stay. By volunteering to clean during lock out in exchange for a free night's accommodation, we were both able to stay much longer in locations throughout our travels around the world. In general, hostels are either run by the owners or by traveler volunteers, so it never hurts to ask if they could use the extra help in exchange for a free night's rent!

Kim

While I can't recall who suggested this (money saving) tip to me on my very first backpacking trip in Europe, I do remember wondering if I was possibly being punked. I'll admit to being nervous the first time I offered my help at a hostel in Glasgow, Scotland, but was quickly put at ease when they gladly accepted. This decision resulted in me staying an extra couple of nights when I would have otherwise left as originally planned. After that first experience, I began to ask every hostel owner or manager I met (in towns or cities I thought were cool) if they needed volunteer support during the busy season. At one hostel in Switzerland, I helped for so many weeks that I ended up being offered the only single bedroom, and was able to move out of the dorms. While in many ways, working throughout my travels slowed my journey, I was better able to savor the places and people I met along the way. The bonus of my decision was that I saved so much money that summer while backpacking in Europe that I was able to roll that savings into a trip around the world, just six months later!

Sheet and Towel Rentals

Every now and then you will come across a hostel that does not freely provide bedding and requires you to rent their bed sheets or towels, assuming you didn't bring your own (which most places don't encourage—again, bedbugs). While not necessarily an expensive add-on, it's worth mentioning since these rentals can eat into your daily budget, especially if you're accounting for every dollar spent.

This information can nearly always be found on the hostel booking page, but we recommend reading the reviews or asking when you call or walk in. Regardless, even if renting a towel is an available option, we still recommend packing a small microfiber travel towel for your journey. These are quick drying, come in multiple sizes, and pack surprisingly small. From daily showers to waterfall swims to makeshift blankets, you'd be surprised how often they will come in handy.

Sleeping Bags & Sleep Sacks

Consider the following: if your travels will span several countries or if you plan to camp at any point, and if you're willing to invest in an ultra-lightweight, warm, high-tech sleeping bag that can pack down super small and live at the bottom of your pack (just in case), then it's worth considering. If, however, you are staying in major cities and don't plan on getting too rural, then you can forgo the expense and loss of pack space. Just to distinguish, sleep sacks (not to be confused with sleeping bags) are ultra-thin, often made of 100% silk, and pack down to about the size of a soda can. These are great to have when traveling through hot climates or during the summer as not all hostels have air conditioning.

Here are some examples of when a sleeping bag may or may not prove necessary or useful.

* **Trekking the foothills of the Himalayas?**
  Having your own sleeping bag in addition to the blankets they provide is a wise choice. Personal experience taught us that asking for an additional blanket meant our guide went without.

* **Walking the Camino de Santiago de Compostela?**
  Pack a sleeping bag—between rustic albergues and cooler evening temps, you'll be grateful for the extra comfort and warmth. Trust us, a sarong won't be enough in early spring or late fall.

* **Backpacking through eastern Europe?**
  All the hostels will likely have plenty of blankets to go around so leave your sleep sack tucked away.

* **Going off the beaten path in the Atacama Desert?**
  That sleeping bag may come in handy again.

Snoring

- In shared dorms, it is best to accept that being kept up by snoring as an inevitability. At some point a bunkmate will snore.
- If you never encounter a snoring bunkmate, there is a good chance that it's you. The easiest fix to avoid sleepless nights is to travel with a pair of reusable foam ear plugs in your pack.

Kim

For many years, the Sleep Master Sleep Mask was my personal favorite for traveling; in fact I still use this mask at home to block ambient light and sound to get a good night's sleep when my husband snores. Regardless of the brand, be sure to choose one that is 100% silk, wraps fully around your head, covers your ears, and secures flat against your head with Velcro (no thin elastic strings) to block out all light for a blissful night's sleep. These are great for catching some z's on planes, trains, or in eight-person hostel dorms! Another brand-specific option that I like is Loop earplugs. They look like gauges in your ears, come in different styles and materials, are low profile, and are great for sound dampening or silencing (depending on the style you purchase). Bonus, they actually look cool! Not only are they great for sleeping but they come in handy if trying to preserve your later-in-life hearing when clubbing the night away at a European discotheque!

Failing that, a pair of music earbuds can often do the trick, though be mindful to set the volume of your music low enough to not disturb your bunkmates, especially if your noise cancelling setting is active.

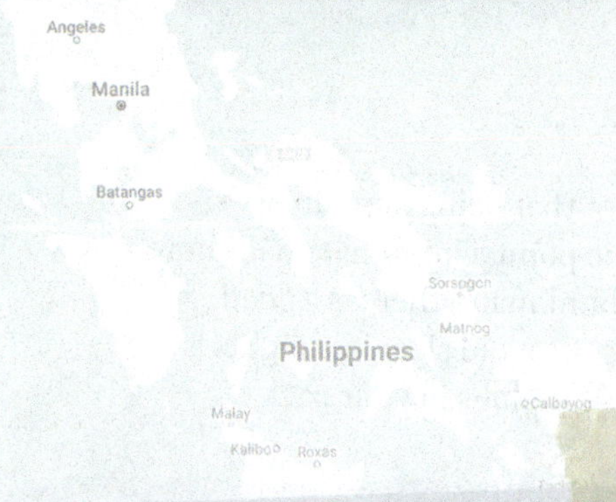
Angeles
Manila
Batangas
Sorsogon
Matnog
Philippines
Malay
Calbayog
Kalibo
Roxas

Alarm Clocks

If you are the type of person who can sleep through any alarm clock sound or hits snooze a thousand times, we guarantee your bunkmates will hate you. Fret not, there are plenty of products that can wake you by alternative means, such as a watch that vibrates or Bose sleepbuds that have a built-in alarm feature. Just be sure to practice using (and responding to) these products in advance. The night before an early flight is not the time to test them for the first time! One thing you will develop by staying in hostels is a sensitivity to sounds, both soothing and disturbing. Use this to your advantage and set your alarm to the least disruptive volume that will wake you up but not everyone else.

Alternatively, you can grant permission to someone in your dorm to shake you awake or throw things at you if you don't wake up to your alarm after the first two snoozes. We assure you if you don't silence your alarm, they will want to do that anyway!

Common Rooms & Mindful Manners

We want you to make new friends and maybe have a few flings everywhere you go, however it's rude and disrespectful to your fellow bunkmates to stay up all night chatting across your bunk. Hostels provide common rooms for this very interaction. Find a quiet place away from neighboring dorm rooms and be mindful of your volume as the night turns to day.

PRO-TIP

Don't have access to fancy gadgets or alarms? Investing in a cheap digital (not smart) watch with an alarm feature will generally do the trick. Considering most bunk beds have iron frames, wrapping your watch band around the headboard near your ear is an easy alarm clock hack that you won't drop off the top bunk when you reach for it in the dark. You don't want to solely rely on your phone and risk oversleeping (thereby missing your train or plane the next morning) because your phone didn't charge properly overnight and died.

As a Rule of Thumb = Common rooms are for communing. + Sleeping rooms are for sleeping!

We've both been there. An overnight flight arrived early but check in to the hostel isn't available until the afternoon. Later you are finally granted access to your bed, able to lie down after thirty hours of straight travel, only to have a few people come into the room intent on hanging out and chatting loudly. Don't be that guy! Hostels are designed with ample common room options for you to hang out and chat, allowing other travelers to rest in their assigned dorms. Traveling takes a lot of sustained energy and having a quiet place to rest is vital to enjoying your trip in good health.

Do not treat the dorm room as your own personal hotel room, because it's not. For example, if you're catching an early flight, train, or bus the next day, nothing will make fellow travelers resent you faster than rustling plastic bags and rummaging around the room blindly in the wee hours. If you have an early exit planned, pack your bag the night before with everything you need for the morning laid out with space left in the top of your pack for anything you need to repack.

There is simply no reason to separate all your worldly possessions into multiple plastic shopping or resealable bags!! While there are packing systems that help keep things organized, they're usually better suited for suitcases and not backpacks. At best, one reusable bag designated for dirty laundry is really all you need. If your organizational habits really require you to separate your items, try mesh zipper bags instead. These can also be used to keep delicate or small items from getting lost or destroyed in the wash.

PRO-TIP

Instead of (bad for the environment) disposable (and loud) plastic shopping bags, consider investing in some inexpensive and reusable packable bags. Chico bags are a personal favorite of ours. They're super strong, washable, reusable, and fit a shit-ton of stuff in them. If you're looking for a water or leak-proof option for liquids you might be carrying and worry might spill, you can invest in some inexpensive, resealable silicone bags. They come in many sizes and, unlike their disposable counter parts, are soft and make very little noise.

Common Bathrooms

Most hostels will have shared bathrooms with varying degrees of style and privacy. If you have preferences or specific needs, it's best to consult the hostel website and read reviews in advance.

Below are some examples of what some hostel shared bathrooms can include.

- ★ Fully enclosed single stalls
- ★ Coed or single-sex bathrooms
- ★ One bathroom per dorm (en suite)
- ★ Shared bathrooms for each floor
- ★ Shared bathrooms for the entire facility

Other Shower Considerations to Mention

Save your spare change. Some hostel showers are coin-operated, which help limit water usage and mitigate someone hogging all the hot water. Pack shower flip-flops or other sandals that you are happy getting wet and wear them into the shower with you. This is completely optional. Most hostels are squeaky clean, and this is really an individual preference, but if you're the last one in the shower that day, your feet may thank you. Find out what time the showers get cleaned each day so you can plan accordingly and be the first one to get a sparkling fresh shower experience.

Be sure to take your towel, toiletries, and any clothing you'll want post-shower in with you so all you'll need to do is dry off and get dressed in the stall.

PRO-TIP

Showering just after a lock out has ended is a great way to ensure you're getting the cleanest shower opportunity possible!

Natasha

I won't admit that I have had to run naked across a hostel lobby soaking wet and partially wrapped in an old T-shirt, but I'm also not prepared to deny it.

Toilets

Hostel toilets and the availability of toilet paper are culturally specific. Don't assume based on where you're from. Be sure to research the regions you'll be traveling through ahead of time. While you likely won't find yourself without TP in western Europe, most of Southeast Asia has squat toilets and buckets of water in lieu of toilet paper or a flushing mechanism. In Brazil, Greece, and many islands the septic systems cannot accommodate flushing of toilet paper (or anything at all) and will have a trash bin to discard paper or sanitary products. Japanese toilets can be so fancy that it's like visiting a day spa for your tush.

Laundry

Just about every hostel has an option for laundry. Some have coin-operated machines; others are more rustic and offer a handwashing station with an iron hand crank roller to thread your clothing through to squeeze out excess water before hanging them to dry. Keep in mind, not all hostels will offer laundry detergent, so it's best to travel with a small bag of dry detergent (liquid is heavier) or an all-inclusive alternative like Dr. Bronners, which is good for handwashing clothes on the go as well as washing your hair, body, and teeth.

✈ PRO-TIP

It should go without saying, but do not flush anything other than toilet paper down a toilet (assuming it's permitted). Sanitary products, tampons, or even flushable wipes will wreak havoc on a septic system. If extra TP is available, kindly wrap these items and discretely place them in the bin. Remember, you are a guest and may need to adjust your bathroom etiquette per the country you are exploring. Finally, a pocket pack of tissues can double as emergency TP in situations where nature may call you unexpectedly or the toilet conditions aren't what you're accustomed to. If you're in nature or in a place where tossing paper or products isn't permitted, this is when one of your resealable silicone bags can be a temporary stash spot until you can properly dispose of them.

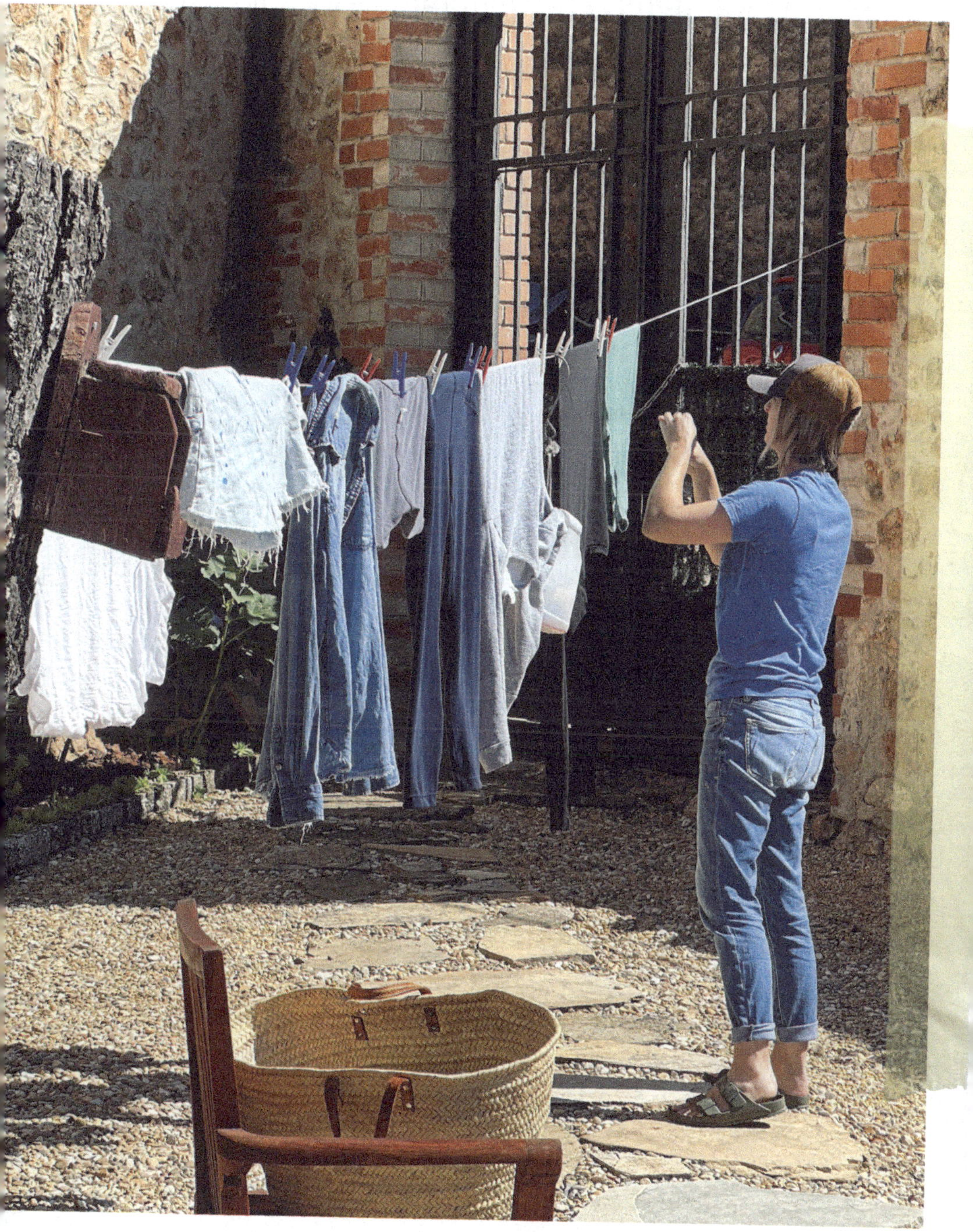

Common Kitchens & Remember, Your Mother Doesn't Live Here

Like the heart of many homes, hostel kitchens can be an educational gateway to international culinary cuisine and bonding with people from other cultures. Travelers from all over the world will cook their countries' cuisines and comfort foods in hostel kitchens. If food is offered, be willing to try their cooking and similarly offer the food you've created to cross cultural culinary borders.

Collaborate with other travelers and create something new and exciting together! It's amazing how many versions of curry you can make with random ingredients! Not only will you sharpen your cooking skills, but you will practice sustainability by not wasting or over purchasing ingredients that might otherwise go to waste for a simple recipe. What may seem like a simple snack to you could be a gateway culinary experience to someone else. Generally speaking, most hostel kitchens will have basic shared provisions such as salt, pepper, and oil as well as cooking utensils and cutlery.

Natasha

One of my favorite memories is that each night a different person in the dorm would cook a meal for everyone from their home country.

As we mentioned earlier regarding lock out periods for cleaning, unlike hotels, most hostels are not staffed with a professional cleaning crew to pick up after you. Hostels are typically minimally staffed with volunteer travelers exchanging two to three hours of work for a free night's accommodation (we highly recommend this option if you're traveling on the cheap) and maybe one or two paid staff members or an owner. Please don't intentionally make their job harder. You never know, but that other backpacker in the kitchen making spaghetti with you may very well be the one responsible for cleaning it later. At the end of the day be respectful of everyone and clean up after yourself.

PRO-TIP

Pack a marker and label your food! While this may seem like petty behavior to some, it is paramount in shared hostel kitchens to help differentiate your supply of pasta, sauce, and peanut butter from those of the other twelve travelers sharing the fridge. Use a marker to name and date all food you leave in the shared kitchen. The general rule of thumb is if there is no name, or the date is more than a week old, it's fair game for anyone to eat. Although, if prepared food is more than a week old, it may be best to forgo your late-night munchies.

In summary, name your food, take your shit, and keep things clean. If you see a name and date on food and it's not yours, don't eat it! It's that simple.

No (Bunk) Bed Available?

First and foremost, don't despair. Also, we never said backpacking would be glamorous, and sometimes you may not find yourself sleeping in a bed. Collectively, we have slept in train stations; airports; en route in a bus, ferry, plane, and train; once on a park bench until a kind local took pity and then on a lumpy futon; floors; a thin mat on the floor; an itchy thatch of hay in a barn; an attic; hammocks; and once in an assigned tent on the back lawn of a New Zealand hostel that served as "overflow" lodging, not to be confused with camping.

If you're planning to travel in your destination's high season, such as summer in Europe, winter in South America, or Christmas in India or Australia, be sure to have a backup accommodations plan. Having a general idea or being willing to ask around for more than one hostel recommendation and having their contact information handy should you need to reach out is a good idea.

When you arrive in a new city, you may feel overwhelmed and a bit disoriented. Don't forget to take a moment to breathe and gather your bearings. Swing by the local tourist destination center (usually located near central train stations), grab a city map, then maybe stop in a cafe to enjoy a flat white (coffee with milk) and get a handle of the landscape before embarking on a hostel hunt. If the first hostel doesn't have availability, ask them for a referral to a nearby alternative. Some hostels have multiple locations in town. Most hostels have a storage room for bags. If you ask nicely, they may allow you to leave your bag there while you continue your quest for accommodations. ➙

This will not only ease your shoulders but keep you from looking vulnerable while becoming acquainted with the city.

Keep in mind the time of day you're trying to book. As we've explained regarding lock outs, most hostels close their reception desks from anywhere between 10:00 a.m. and 5:00 p.m., when cleaning, servicing, and maintenance takes place. If you're walking the Camino de Santiago, municipal hostels or albergues will have you out the door by 8:30a.m. While certain hostels allow for backpackers to access their rooms during this lock out time of day, others do not. Make sure you ask and are aware of any rules as they vary from hostel to hostel.

If you're trying to contact a hostel to find out about same-day reservations during a lock out period, simply leave a message and contact info where you can be reached. This can sometimes be a gamble as you may find out at 5:05 p.m. that there's no room at the inn. If there is another hostel in the city or town you're exploring, work your way down the list. Sometimes arriving in person looking forlorn and weary works in your favor, but not always, so bear that in mind.

If you believe you may arrive in a city any later than the afternoon, it is suggested to book at least your first night's accommodations prior to arrival, even if it is just a few hours beforehand.

Natasha

I acquired an almost secret piece of information while I was working (in a somewhat ambiguous legal gray-area) in a European hostel. A great many of hostels in Europe will not accept walk-ins past approximately 5:00 p.m. (this will likely never be an issue anywhere in Asia). This is done in many major cities to prevent drunk locals from simply booking a room when they become too intoxicated to drive home. They want to keep their backpackers safe, and this requires certain rules to keep out the riff raff. As the receptionist I was told to simply say "We are fully booked for this evening."

Couch Surfing – Friends You Haven't Met Yet

Travel the World.
Rediscover your City.
Become a Host.

—Couch Surfing motto

If you find yourself without a room in a one-hostel-town (it's rare but happens), becoming a verified member of an organization such as Couch Surfing can be an amazing way to supplement your accommodations options. Couch surfers can offer you a clean couch or whole room to yourself and, in many instances, a travel-friendly local tour guide willing to show you around their hometown. Becoming a couch surfing member doesn't require you to sleep on someone's couch. At the very least, it's a safe way to connect with locals in a strange new city, town, or country, and can be as casual as meeting up for a beer or coffee, or as adventurous as meeting up to rock climb at the local gym. ➜

Essentially once you sign up, complete the profile, and pay the fee for verification, you're a certified member able to connect with like-minded community members within your hometown and abroad. Paying to have your account verified as well as seeking out verified profiles is a visible, safe, and easy way to instill trust that you are who you say you are, as is the person you might meet up with. This is an infinite resource for information whether you actually meet anyone in person or not. Considering you're not confirmed as verified until you receive your Couch Surfing postcard at the specified address of verification, it's best to complete this necessary step prior to embarking on your adventures.

With Couch Surfing, safety and security are high priorities with care and consideration taken to ensure each member and host has been screened and verified. Referrals, ratings, and references assist in keeping this system of checks and balances in place. Despite these safety features, it's always advised to meet fellow couch surfers first in a public setting to get a feel or sense of the individual to intuit if you (both) feel comfortable with moving forward with accommodations. While 99% of all experiences are positive, outliers do exist. For safety basics and tips, review the list on their website. In short, hone your bullshit radar and stay safe!

Couch surfing is also a great meetup tool for travelers who want to host but do not have the space to spare and yet are happy to meet for a drink or a guided walk-about. With twelve-million members in 200,000 cities hosting 550,000 events, it's a great resource for travelers and locals alike. Check out...

www.couchsurfing.com

for more information.

Natasha

I was once genuinely rescued by a couch surfer host. After a long day of hitchhiking from Ushuaia, Argentina, toward southern Chile, I found myself, along with two other hitchhikers who'd joined me along the way, stuck in a border town. The sun was beginning to depart, the cold set in, and mild panic began to weigh on us. There were no hostels and only one hotel that was blatantly beyond our price range.

We opted to walk miles to a healthcare facility, as they provided Wi-Fi, and began messaging every couch surfing host we could find. In a stroke of luck, a man drove by the curb we were sitting on and called out our names. In sheer bewilderment we realized that he was one of the recipients of our pleas just moments prior. He'd noticed our distress and declared that he had noticed the message while driving. As he had just passed three backpackers looking distraught and wildly out of place, he just assumed that it must be us. It took us by surprise but, fresh out of options, we climbed into his small SUV. He drove us four blocks to his house where he proceeded to provide us with shelter, showers, entertainment, and a home-cooked meal.

After dinner we became bewildered when he stepped out, trusting us alone in his apartment. He later returned to surprise us with what can only be described as the most delicious ice cream available on the planet! This act of love and kindness only instilled in me that there are still wonderful people in this world willing to open their hearts and homes to complete strangers.

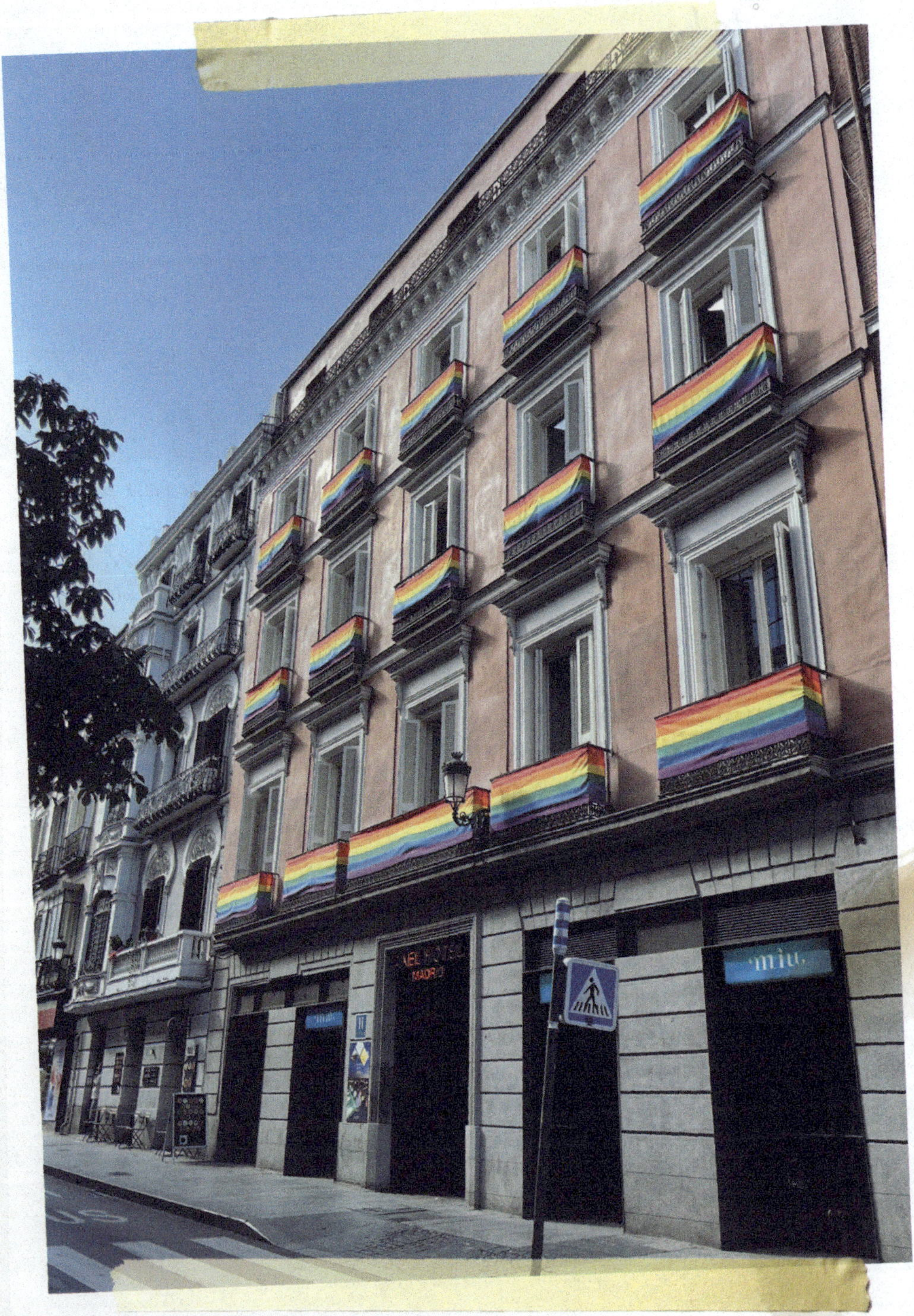
miu

Airbnb & Vrbo

Airbnbs & Vrbos have arguably become some of the most popular forms of travel accommodations around the world today. With an easy international booking platform and homes for almost every budget all over the world, often at a discount to nearby hotel prices, this is no surprise. We won't deny we love a good Airbnb for a relaxing beach vacation or weekend break from the city with friends.

However, unless the place you are visiting is lacking social hostel options, these kinds of stays wouldn't be our first pick for solo backpackers and here's why:

* Many are a bit off the beaten path and inaccessible by public transport, therefore requiring private transport or paying for ride shares, which can eat into your daily budget. They are isolating and don't naturally allow for the social environment often found in hostels, meaning no new travel friends along the journey!

* While they can be budget friendly, they still tend to cost more than the other options we've outlined. Once you tack on additional fees and taxes, what you've spent in one night could otherwise be applied to alternative accommodations over the course of several nights.

If you have a bit more to spend and prefer the solitude that private accommodations allow, then do what is right for you. As we have said again and again, there is no wrong way to travel, except with a closed mind, and depending on where you find yourself in life when traveling, the additional solitude may be just what you need.

Homestays

A homestay is a more intimate way of travel, typically involving staying with a local family for a nominal fee to experience the regional customs, cuisine, and general way of life firsthand. Homestays can vary from full immersion into a family to being given a spare room and left to your own devices. They can be long-term or for just a night, luxurious or a mud hut (and who's to say that's not luxurious in its own way?). Homestays allow you to peer behind the cultural curtain, so to speak (don't actually peer behind anyone's curtains, please), of everyday life where you're traveling.

We've taken the liberty to outline some pros and cons.

Pros

- Offer an authentic cultural experience
- Allow you to get off the grid
- Budget-friendly
- Family style environment to battle travel loneliness in rural regions
- Experience local cuisine in a family setting
- Provide natural opportunities to learn or hone a new language

Cons

- May lack privacy (and Wi-Fi)
- Can cause culture shock, such as requiring you to closely abide by local customs that you are unaccustomed to
- House rules, such as limiting shower usage or enforcing a curfew

If an opportunity arises where you are invited to spend an extended period of time with a local family, trust your instincts and suss out that it's a safe option, and if it is, don't pass it up. Remember, you have just as much to teach them about who you are and where you come from as you have to learn. The world, despite what you may see and hear on the news, is full of incredible humans with open hearts and minds. Show the world you are as well.

WWOOFing & Farm Stays

If you love digging in the dirt, nuzzling sheep, and getting away from the hustle and bustle of city life, you might want to explore the possibilities of Worldwide Opportunities on Organic Farms (WWOOF). In exchange for free room and board, you will assist a local farmer (of your choosing and depending on their availability and needs) and gain farming experience, expand your knowledge of sustainability, and experience new cultures from a local perspective.

With locations worldwide, this is a great way to get to know a place a bit better and learn practical skills or develop a self-sufficient lifestyle. Farm experiences range from picking fruit and veg to working with animals and everything in between. With urban and rural options for WWOOF around the world, it's a unique opportunity to get off the beaten path and really dig into the local culture. Pun intended! Detailed farm listings and guidebooks are distributed by country and region, so go online to learn more. For a one-stop shop for links to any country of interest, visit the WWOOF website.

Camping

Tent camping, car camping, and glamping are great options in a lot of countries, especially if you'll be traveling by car, including but not limited to:

- ☆ Australia
- ☆ New Zealand
- ☆ Central and South America
- ☆ Iceland
- ☆ North America
- ☆ Southeast Asia
- ☆ India (glamping in particular)

If you're considering camping, you might also be considering a backpacker vehicle of some kind. We talk about this in chapter three. Instead of renting a vehicle and getting caught up in the headache that entails, look for a used car from a backpacker traveler who's ready to move on. Hostel bulletin boards in major cities are your best bet for these connections, but there are web resources too.

Depending on the country, you can score one that's already stocked with all the camping gear you'll need, including but not limited to a tent, stove, plates and cutlery, and sleeping bag. We'd still recommend traveling with your own sleeping bag to avoid the possible spread of bedbugs and also guarantee that you'll be warm when the evening temps drop. Then when you're ready to move on, sell the vehicle to the next adventure seeker and recoup a little cash. Win. Win. Win.

If you're planning to car camp (car, van, bus, or tent), find out if free camping is permitted in the region you will be visiting. This may afford you the opportunity to pull over and pitch your tent in whatever beautiful locale you may currently find yourself. A great compromise between social and solo traveling is to alternate between camping and staying in hostels. You may also find another solo backpacker, up for the adventure, that you want to camp with for a while.

During high seasons, when hostel beds may be in high demand, see if the hostel has a backyard or garden where they might allow you to pitch your tent. This can offer a safe and social alternative if the next campsite is 50 kilometers away and it's getting late. Also, since so many hostels have kitchens, hot showers, laundry, and sometimes a small convenience store, it's a great way to regroup before hitting the road again and maybe meet a new travel companion while you're waiting for your laundry to dry! Regardless of how you choose to enjoy the great outdoors, fancy or free, plan your route accordingly to ensure you will be near public or fee- based camp or caravan grounds.

Hotels

We have listed hotels last by design. The opportunities for friends, adventure, and budget- savings are just not available in the same way if you select to stay only in hotels. There can be a time and place for hotels, near an airport the night before a big flight for example, but generally they will cause your trip to be more expensive, significantly less fun and, at times, downright lonely.

It is also common for people back home—such as your parents, relatives, their nosy friends (we both experienced this more than once), your friends, or even your employer—to tell you that you're crazy to stay in a hostel, homestay, or to couch surf, or even that you're crazy for traveling (alone) in general! Don't believe them! With all their well-meaning efforts of misguided good intention, they'll claim that you are much safer in a hotel than any of those other alternatives we've outlined in such loving detail. We're going to defy all their good intentions and boldly tell you that they are wrong. To rveiterate, occasionally hotels are fine, but you didn't leave the comfort of your home, by yourself, to sit in a hotel room by yourself.

A Summary of Why We Prefer Hostels or Homestays Over Hotels

Hostels:
Pros

- Lots of other solo travelers to keep you company and notice if you don't return
- Easy to make friends to travel with to your next destination
- Lots of other travelers to join you for a night out, exploring the city, figuring out public transport, and more
- Staff is made up of other travelers and they will let you know of local pitfalls to look out for and tips to keep you safe
- They notice if you don't return (we know, harp, harp, harp, but hey, we were and are women who often travel alone—personal safety is of high regard—ours and yours!)
- Often offer group activities around the city, such as pub crawls or sightseeing tours, so that you don't have to wander the city alone, unless you choose to
- Closed to the public—while each hostel is different, they all commonly only allow people staying in the hostel to come into the hostel facilities with rare exceptions in some smaller villages around the world. This is often further enforced by a staff buzzer or a lock and key to the front entrance

Homestays/Couch Surfing/WWOOFing:
Pros

- Locals host you who know the ropes of the town
- You make new friends
- Hosts are often former or future backpackers who understand the wanderlust you're experiencing
- Couch surfers create public profiles that, once verified, ensure safety and security that they are who they say they are; again, it's always advised to meet first in a public setting to get a feel or sense of the individual to intuit if you (both) feel comfortable providing or accepting accommodations
- A family/friends to keep an eye on you
- People who notice if you don't return in the evening
- Not open to the public

Hotels: Pros

* They can offer the occasional quiet, restful, and rejuvenating night's sleep—remember traveling for an extended period can be energetically draining, so it's important to rest as needed throughout your journey
* They can be a convenient option close to the airport if you arrived late or have an early flight out and don't have a lot of time to spare
* Sometimes they are the only, or safer, option in a remote area—especially when a hostel is not an available option

Hotels: Cons

* They're isolating and lonely and while they can afford you a solid night's sleep, so can a private room in a public hostel where you still are in the social sphere of international travelers
* They're (more) expensive and will eat faster into your daily budgeted allowance
* Attendants and guests can see that you have checked in and are staying alone. It's unlikely a hotel staff member would check to see if you returned safely in the evening
* Fancier hotels may even have restaurants and bars that are open to the public and they don't monitor who comes and goes. While this could be considered a pro item, this again presents a safety concern when traveling alone that is easily remedied by staying in hostels more geared toward the independent backpacker

Staying Safe

Regardless of which option you pick, the primary goal is to be sure you have a safe place to rest your head at night.

Here are a few more tips:

- **Tell Someone Where You're Staying –** If you're trying something new (couch surfing, WWOOFing, camping, etc.), share the name and location of your accommodations with friends or family back home or with fellow travelers as you move from place to place until you get your traveler's feet under you and fine-tune your no-bullshit radar. Parents and especially those that love you will worry regardless of how safe we say it is, so put their minds at ease and let them know where you're staying from time to time. Trust us, that small show of consideration means more to those back home than we can truly articulate.

- **Read the Reviews –** While we'd never encourage you to take a Yelp review at face value (we get it, everyone is a foodie), we do encourage you to research and review hostels. You and future travelers will benefit from these insights. Mostly you're looking for cleanliness, proximity to attractions or transportation, and overall good vibes!

- **Trust Your Instincts –** If something feels off, find another place. Period. Don't stick it out. If you don't feel comfortable, leave!

- **Carry a Combination Lock –** Many hostels assign lockers or chests in which to keep your belongings or smaller lockers in which to keep valuables. Some places will provide locks, and some will have locks to rent, but we always suggest keeping a small combination lock with you just in case. Protect your shit! Especially documents and your passport!

WHEREVER I LAY MY HAT THAT'S MY HOME

* **Remember Karma –**
  Don't take anyone else's stuff (not even their phone charger or food from the fridge) without asking permission. In all situations, apply the golden rule and when in doubt, ask.
* **Be A Gracious Guest –**
  At the end of the day, be a gracious and considerate guest regardless if you're paying to stay or accepting the generosity of those who will take you in along your journey. Let your host know if you aren't planning on returning that evening. While calling to check in may feel like you are back at home, hostel staff and other hosts genuinely care and worry about you and, as you'll discover, you will worry about them.
* **Don't Overstay Your Welcome –**
  If you are fortunate enough to be extended a place to stay by a fellow traveler or local, keep in mind in almost all settings that houseguests are like fish and after three days they start to stink. Realizing in hindsight that you've overstayed your welcome can be a humbling embarrassment.

PETRA

10
Bucket List Ideas
To check off your list

51. Join a spice tour in Zanzibar .... ☐
52. Check out an arts festival in Kraków, Poland. .... ☐
53. Visit an underground jazz club in Prague, Czech Republic ..... ☐
54. Swim in crystal blue waters in Bali, Indonesia .... ☐
55. Sip tea in a traditional ceremony in Kyoto, Japan .... ☐
56. Sing karaoke in Seoul, South Korea .... ☐
57. Drink yak's milk in the Gobi in Mongolia .... ☐
58. Harvest grapes in Bordeaux, France. .... ☐
59. Visit the ancient city of Petra, Jordan .... ✈☐
60. Walk around the Red Square in Moscow, Russia. .... ☐

7
DON'T BE THAT GAL

I am intensely grateful for the kindness, hospitality, and patience the people of West Virginia showed to this ignorant rube from New York City who arrived with so many of the usual preconceptions, only to have them turned on their head.

—Anthony Bourdain, Parts Unknown Field Notes

Ethnocentrism is an anthropological term defined as an evaluation of other cultures according to preconceptions originating in the standards and customs of one's own culture. It often coincides with the belief that one's own ethnicity, race, religion, or personal customs are superior to another. In layman's terms, ethnocentrism is judging another culture based on the beliefs created in your own culture. It assumes that the other culture is wrong or inferior simply because their customs or beliefs do not align with your own.

For example, a traveler goes to a country and observes that husbands and fathers do not participate in household chores or child rearing. If the traveler grew up in a Western culture, they may deem this behavior as a negative. They may even think of these men as bad fathers or husbands. They tell themselves they would never put up with this or act in such a way. They don't realize that the particular culture being judged may have more defined and separated gender roles, where men must work and women must stay home and raise children. Be careful in how quickly you judge what you do not yet understand. ➡

We should not judge another's way of life as inferior or less loving or respectful without taking into consideration the culture's own personal customs. That wife may feel that she is very lucky to have such a prosperous husband who works so her family can afford the luxury of food and a home (something not everyone in their area may have) and he may deem himself a successful and loving man for doing so. It is not for us to judge, especially without first considering a culture's feelings, customs, and beliefs as well as the personal situation.

Similar to the aforementioned examples, the same judgment can be applied to religion. Wars as old as time have been waged over this very topic, and there are those who have made it their life's work to travel the world and introduce usually nomadic or tribal cultures to their version of religious-based beliefs. To assume that individuals around the world have prayed or worshiped incorrectly for centuries is culturally ignorant and further prohibits understanding, growth, and global unity.

As you can see from the examples above, ethnocentrism is not always obvious and your concerns regarding another culture may not always be valid, necessary, or even warranted. It is not for us as travelers to judge what is right or wrong without first considering that specific culture's history, customs, and beliefs as well as the personal situation you find yourself in or observing. Be a curious traveler. Ask respectful questions. Above all, observe, listen, and do not assume that what is different is wrong.

Remember, we are merely passing shadows and should approach our experiences with a sense of curiosity and observation. As travelers, it is our social responsibility to reserve judgment and approach other cultures with an open mind (and heart), eager to learn and grow through the experiences gifted, shared, or created by those we encounter along the way.

Natasha

I traveled to India with what I believed was an open mind. I immersed myself in the culture. I tasted the local delicacies, danced at the festivals, and observed religious practices respectfully and happily. It wasn't until a conversation with a young Indian girl over a mango lassi in the coastal city of Goa that I learned otherwise. We spoke about our lives, and she revealed that she was awaiting a marriage arrangement. I did not openly express my disdain for the practice, but she could sense my pity and opened the floor for a dialogue on the situation, asking why I appeared bothered.

Per my cultural identity, I shared my beliefs on being in control of your own destiny and the idea of romantic love. I then noticed that she began to pity me. Confused, I asked her to explain how she felt about the situation. She expressed that she felt she was very lucky she could enjoy her life in leisure, go to school, spend time with her friends, and just relax knowing that her parents would find her a suitable mate. That the love in her marriage would grow over time based on mutual respect and understanding. She actually felt sorrow toward my situation and the uncertainty of my future; would I find a suitable husband or end up alone? She could not fathom the stress put forth during dating, effort put forth into appearances, and the heartache I may endure if I were to select the wrong mate.

Religion and Politics

We'll keep this short and sweet as the same advice from above should be applied here. Do not assume you are an expert in matters of cultural religion or politics when you are not. Discussion and debate are healthy and afford us an opportunity to better understand cultural differences. It is wise to not interject when your opinion was not called into question. We must not presume to understand another person or people's histories, traditions, politics, rituals, ceremonies, or beliefs. As a traveler, it is best to tread lightly where these topics are concerned and remember that you are an observer. Similarly, we're not discounting your personal history, traditions, politics, rituals, ceremonies or beliefs; however, as a world traveler you're both a cultural observer and an ambassador of yourself, your heritage, and your home country. While avoiding harm, we should always explore with curiosity, dignity, and respect.

If you find yourself pressed for an opinion that you'd rather not share or in a mixed company where someone is trying to get your goat, your best option is to respectfully remove yourself from the conversation. You can say you need to get a drink, go to the bathroom, or simply stretch your legs--by the time you return, the topic will have likely changed.

Kim

During my time in Mongolia, I observed that Buddhism was the most practiced religion with Shamanism being the oldest. You see evidence of this in the ornate temples and shrines throughout the region. A large section of the population, however, is nonreligious, leaving an open door for missionaries from around the world to travel to the region and try to convert the locals. While just over 2% of the population currently identifies as Christian, I discovered during my travels in the early 2000's that Mormonism was the fastest growing religion due to the ambitious campaign of traveling missionaries. When speaking with locals, I found out that a growing concern was that many of the Mongol ceremonies, practices, and traditions were being lost to religious conversion.

It wasn't until I was in the Ulaanbaatar airport that I experienced this missionary intrusion firsthand. Two gentlemen, also awaiting an outbound flight, and I proceeded to have a casual chat, sharing an overview of our experiences in Mongolia. It turned out they had been on a month's long missionary trip, spreading the Word of God to the nomadic Mongols (not taking into consideration their spiritual identification, customs or rituals). Abruptly, and without preamble, one of the men handed me a pamphlet and proceeded to ask if my soul was safe and if it had been touched by the Word of God. Despite no intention of malice, I felt affronted and passionately pissed off. Spirituality and the idea of God had become a personal and precarious concept to me over the years and it was none of this man's damn business!

I found myself reflecting on that experience and the presumption of what is considered the right religion for years after. As someone who at the time still identified as religious, but whose fervor was on the brink of waning, I remember thinking that if I felt aggressively intruded upon, one can assume others around the world feel the same when well-meaning missionaries come to convert them without ever considering an entire people's personal histories and spiritual dogma.

Instead of embracing another culture's ways of worshiping with a curious mind and dignified respect, cultural strangers infer that what others practice is wrong and assume that what they teach is inherently right. From this experience, and others, I've continuously tried to remind myself that the beauty of understanding is not in celebrating our similarities but in discovering our differences. That's why I travel.

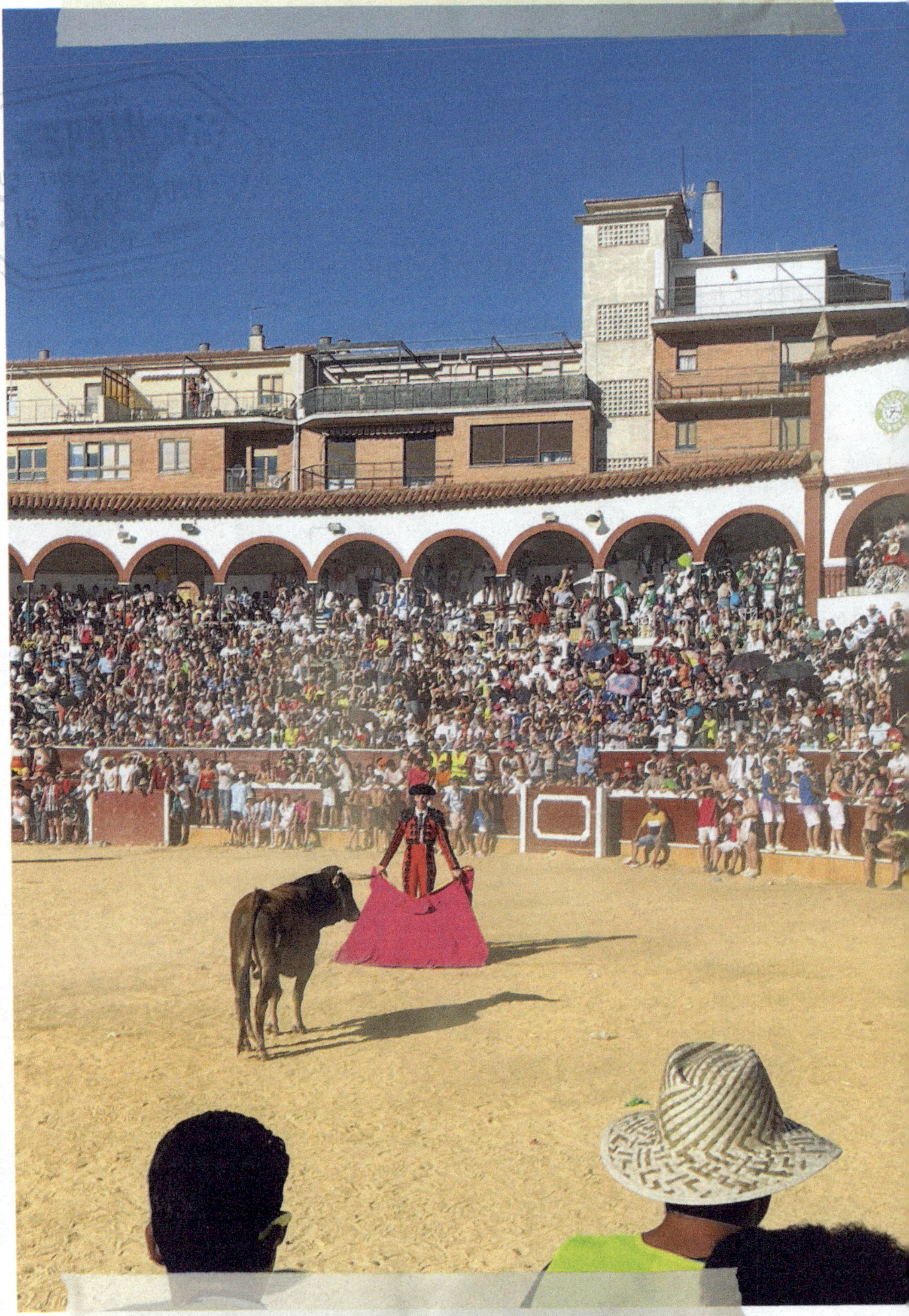

Respect & Cultural Courtesies

Traveling through other countries can be likened to hiking the Appalachian Trail -- leave no trace and take only memories. It should go without saying but we'll say it anyway: respecting other cultures is of paramount importance when traveling. Without overstating the obvious, you are a guest in these countries and should treat the privilege as such and act accordingly. Besides behaving like an ass and giving others from your home country a bad reputation on a global scale, there are few things that can lead you into danger more quickly than culturally pissing off the locals.

Most examples of cultural inappropriateness usually include a fair amount of alcohol and improper social behavior at a bar, pub, or restaurant and are often attributed to just being obnoxious and loud. Other examples stem from a presumption, entitlement, or ignorance that locals should be more accommodating, and you shouldn't have to make as great of an effort as you actually should. Sadly, this perpetuates stereotypes that many foreigners have to work against when traveling. Try not to channel your inner frat-party persona while exploring exotic destinations. It's not a good look, home or abroad.

One easy way to be quickly accepted among the locals while out at the pub or in a local shop is to commit five local-language words or phrases to memory, such as:

- Hello
- My name is...
- How much?
- Thank you
- Where is...?

Write these down on a piece of paper (phonetically) and keep them in your pocket, purse, journal, or travel belt for easy reference. This small effort to say thank you in Czech while having your caricature drawn on the Charles Bridge in Prague will mean more to those you meet than you can comprehend while reading this. Don't assume everyone does or should know your native language. Make an effort every day and see how many unforeseen opportunities present themselves because of it.

Hand gestures are another way you can culturally step in it. This can be as simple as how you count on your fingers when you're trying to indicate how many of an item you'd like to purchase (the French use the thumb as one) to thinking you're giving the peace sign when you're actually telling someone to fuck off.

Not every cultural mishap is acceptable or without serious repercussions. For example, if you didn't research proper tipping etiquette or are drunkenly rude to your server and forget your purse at the restaurant, they may not be inclined to return your bag (with your passport and cash), potentially landing you in a seriously compromised situation.

Public Displays of Affection

Public displays of affection, especially for women, are another gray area that you will want to be clear about when traveling in certain regions throughout the world. While it might be perfectly polite to casually kiss your partner or friend in the West, in other places on this planet, this seemingly benign act can have grave consequences. Sometimes the consequence is so dire it can lead to fines, jail time, or even deportation.

For example, the United Arab Emirates, UAE, places great emphasis on modesty and decency laws, including but not limited to prohibiting public displays of affection for those in relationships or even married. As reported by the BBC, in 2010 a British couple shared a brief kiss in a Dubai restaurant. A local called the police and both were brought to court, prosecuted, fined, and jailed for one month each, before finally being deported. Don't assume your lack of awareness of local laws and customs will exempt you from the consequences.

We share this not to draw negative attention to a specific region, religion, or peoples, but to remind you that not everything that you're used to doing is socially or culturally accepted everywhere around the world and vice versa. Our hope is for you to travel through regions distinctly different from what you know, but with the express understanding of what is culturally acceptable by having done your research ahead of arrival. Various modesties exist throughout this world and will vary greatly within countries and continents.

Interestingly, while many Western countries harbor homophobic stigmas against same-sex individuals holding hands or showing affection, in some Arab, African, Asian, and southern European regions it is both a sign of friendship and respect for people of the same sex (chiefly men) to hold hands with one another. In his best-selling book, Greenlights, Matthew McConaughey shares a profound experience from his time in Africa of being safely escorted, hand in hand, to the next village by a legendary tribesman, after defeating him in an uncontested wrestling match. It was a sign of friendship and respect and a journey he has repeated, hand in hand, more than once. →

If you are fortunate enough to be invited to a local ceremony or performance of any kind, it's worth any detour it may require. Bearing witness to customs or traditions that have likely been passed down for generations in a country of origin is something truly special. As with all events, you're a guest and an observer. Whether you're invited to simply witness or to participate, it's worth mentioning that now is not the time to vlog or livestream your experience, nor is it the time to take a million selfies. You're there to experience things in the moment, not watch it through the barrier of your camera lens. Record the experience without being intrusive and always with permission.

Above all, be present!

Women & Unsolicited Attention

Depending on where you're traveling in the world, women still receive a lot of unwanted attention in the form of sexual harassment. Unlike in many Western countries, women are still considered subservient, second-class citizens, or sexual commodities in some parts of the world. Therefore, modesty isn't just reserved for what you wear but also how you carry yourself in certain regions. Sexual slave trade is still very real and cautionary tales abound.

We highlighted how easy it is to meet like-minded travelers and encourage you to go out in groups in areas you feel may be questionable or unsavory. You will hone your safety instincts along the way, but until you—women, in particular—do, always err on the side of caution. No matter how strong or brave or independent you are (and believe us, you are), remember that the rest of the world might not see you as you see yourself. Therefore, for your safety, it's always advisable to let someone know where you'll be, go out in a group, and ideally not find yourself in a vulnerable position from having too good of a time (getting wasted) at a bar or club. The same safety protocols you would adhere to at home apply abroad! This is yet another reason we encourage staying in hostels as there is nearly always someone to go out with or to tell where you're going. Carry a business card from your hostel in your wallet or purse or write the number down in a small pocket journal in case your phone dies during the night and you need to place an emergency call while you're out. This way, you'll ensure you have the appropriate contact information on hand.

Don't become a cautionary tale. We both have safely traveled to many regions of this world alone. As much as we'd like to claim that we never needed a man, sometimes we would intentionally seek out a trusted (male) traveler we felt comfortable crossing certain borders or exploring less secure regions with. At the end of the day, maybe your bucket list doesn't get completely checked off all on your own and maybe it does. There are plenty of countries we both have held off on visiting due to the simple concern of our individual safety because women are still considered second class citizens. It's not to say these countries are not beautiful and worth visiting one day, but our intention is to keep you safe during your world journeys!

PRO-TIP

Wearing a plain gold or silicone band on your wedding finger can be a visual deterrent against unwarranted male attention while out socially or in a crowded market. Even if you're as single as the day is long, that small symbol can be enough of a deterrent, especially when traveling through certain countries where women's independence is not valued as highly as you value it.

The Power of the Shawl

Modesty is another important factor to consider when choosing a destination. In most Arab cultures shoulders, cleavage, and thighs must be covered while in any public, religious, business, or shopping areas, however a bikini is perfectly acceptable at the more touristy beaches and water parks. For example, in Tel Aviv you can dress the way you would in nearly any European metropolis, but when visiting smaller towns, much more modest dress is required.

Similarly, when visiting structures of worship in Mediterranean countries, shoulder or head coverings may be required or preferred. For most men this isn't a concern (except maybe if wearing a tank top in summer) and is usually resolved by putting on or taking off a hat or cap.

For women, we suggest packing a lightweight scarf, shawl, or sarong and keeping it handy in your purse or day pack for such impromptu moments of modesty. If you find yourself in Greece or Italy having forgotten your shawl, sometimes you can find a basket of scarves at the entrance as a courtesy cover-up for visitors. We suggest traveling with one to show that you're a savvy and respectful explorer already aware of these cultural requests. Just because you happen upon a gorgeous beach off the beaten path doesn't necessarily mean you are welcomed to wear your bikini at it. It's also not to say you can't diminish your tan lines and go topless. When in doubt, always check what's appropriate with your hostel, hotelier, or at the local tourist information center.

Safety!

Confusingly, these particularities and customs are not only dependent on the country you're exploring but the specific city, town, or province you're in as well. For this reason and others, we impart that this is not the time to express your feminist ideals in a form of personal protest. Much like our previous examples regarding cultural acceptance of public displays of affection, your safety could be in jeopardy if you do not respect the local modesty customs. We have no desire for you to find yourself in jail (or worse). We are sharing this from our own personal experiences and in accordance with on-the-ground guidance we both received during our travels.

Upon arrival and on your way to your hostel, look around and ask yourself these questions:

- Do you see any shoulders exposed (tank tops)?
- Is anyone wearing shorts or skirts above the knee?
- Are women covering their heads or faces? →

The Dubai Mall Courtesy Policy

Mall Timings:
Sunday - Wednesday
10:00 am - 10:00 pm

Thursday - Saturday
10:00 am - 12:00 midnight

Please Wear Respectful Clothing
Shoulders and knees should be covered
Thank you for your cooperation

- No kissing or overt display of affection
- No dangerous activities. For example, sports games, rollerblading or skateboarding
- No smoking in the mall
- No pets are allowed in the mall

If the overall answer is no but you're in a non-Western country, it is best to avoid excess skin exposure until you confirm otherwise. You're already prepared with a kick-ass suggested packing list that takes all these scenarios into consideration. If you find yourself immersed in a culture that values modesty or you just aren't sure, fear not! The best advice we have is also the simplest one: always carry a scarf or sarong with you! They can be used as headscarves as well as cover your shoulders or chest.

A light sarong is even valuable to carry in countries that are super cosmopolitan or don't have issues with modesty. Thailand, for example, embraces the itty bitty bikini! You may walk around most areas as exposed as you so choose. However, the gorgeous Buddhist temples require more coverage. Even if you don't find yourself exploring the hidden temples, a sarong can be used as a beach blanket, worn to avoid excess sun exposure, or used as a pillow on a long bus journey.

Additional uses for a sarong include:

- Beach blanket, towel, and swimsuit cover-up – all-in-one – Many cultures outside the United States do not pack a separate beach towel when going to the beach, just a sarong
- Lightweight skirt or scarf – For when it's chilly or to cover up shoulders when visiting churches in the summer when wearing a tank top
- Sun cover-up for when you've had enough exposure (*wash in Rit Dye Sun Aid – SPF 30* laundry additive before you leave home for added sun protection!)
- Thin blanket for hot nights camping under the stars
- Head/face covering alternative, if required
- Makeshift privacy curtain in a hostel bunk bed
- Makeshift privacy curtain for when nature calls on the side of the road

PRO-TIP

Buses in Southeast Asia are notorious for being extremely hot or cold (i.e. either no air-conditioning or the air conditioner on full blast). We advise that you dress in layers and be prepared for all temperature scenarios. A sarong or scarf is ideal to carry around when traveling this region as it can be easily stored and can be used as a blanket or pillow on these journeys.

Luxuries We Take for Granted

If you decide to backpack, whether it's for one month or one year, we suggest taking a moment to let go of assumed expectations you're accustomed to at home. Beyond variations to your diet, sleeping arrangements, and adventures in transportation, it's easy to overlook some of the less obvious comforts you may be used to, including but not limited to ice-cold water.

Below are some examples of luxuries you may go without.

- **Ice** – Americans love ice in their drinks (especially water), and it's not just a Southern thing like sweet tea. Get ready to embrace lukewarm water, beer, and possibly mixed drinks in nearly every foreign city you will visit. While often available upon request, keep in mind where you're traveling. Ice is often made using tap water. In certain regions it's not advisable to drink the local water due to lack of filtration systems or local parasites. Adding ice to your beverage can increase the risk of gastric distress.
- **Flushing Toilets or Free Public Restrooms** – Believe it or not, even in the most cosmopolitan cities in the world (Paris, France, for example) you can still come across some really rudimentary toilet situations, including a privately encased hole in the ground (with two metal footprints to serve as your squat guide) in the cemetery where Jim Morrison's grave rests. Conversely, there are state-of-the-art public restrooms throughout many European cities, however, be prepared to carry around some loose pocket change as many require €0.20 or so to gain access through a gated entrance. These are either cleaned manually throughout the day – ensuring well-stocked restrooms and cleanliness – or, in more rare instances, are so high-tech that after each occupant exits, the stall is washed through an automatic self-cleaning process. Either way, keep some coins in your pocket just in case nature calls. She often demands payment. ➡

- **Toilet Paper** – This is kind of a weird consideration because in most westernized cities, toilet paper is readily available within the stalls of public restrooms, though not always (looking at you, last stall at the club). Similarly, if you plan to travel to developing nations, Asia, or Africa, you may find that in lieu of paper you will be provided with a water hose, bucket of water, or nothing at all. We strongly advise you to carry a travel pack of tissues or wet wipes at least until you acclimate to local toilet customs (looking at you, Japan). We've all been there, drunk at 1:00 a.m. and in a bathroom stall without any toilet paper. Besides a scarf or hat, tissues might be the second most important just-in-case item to have on hand at all times!
- **Expediency & Efficiency** – Most of us live in a world of instant gratification where speed and efficiency are the highest qualifier of success. Food is fast, greetings are immediate, concerns are addressed promptly, transport schedules are (fairly) reliable, and you can confidently map out your activities with precision based on times allotted for each activity. Please, please, please understand that this is not the case in the majority of the world, and that's okay! Every culture you cross paths with will be different and have their own standards of efficiency.
- **The Customer is Always Right...Just Kidding!** – You may have heard stories or even seen it on the Amazing Race: rushed Americans loudly declaring they are unhappy with a received service and therefore refusing to pay. Some people believe they can shout their way into getting what they want (in the United States that's unfortunately a tactic that often works, especially against service industry individuals), but we're here to warn you that it won't get you far while abroad. Try that tactic with a strong Italian airline operator or a Balinese taxi driver and you could very well find yourself ignored, kicked off or out, and possibly even altogether stranded where you stand. Our best advice here is always speak calmly and be patient. Toto, you're not in Kansas anymore.
- **Accurate Transport Schedules** – Just because your ticket states a 1:00 p.m. arrival doesn't mean your plane, train, bus, etc. is getting there on time or (less likely but still possible) hasn't already left! Since we've already gone through all the ways your roll might be slowed, we'll simply remind you that flexibility should not only be your friend but your mantra too.

The point we're trying to make is that not every place you visit will have the luxuries you are accustomed to at home. Therefore, it is unrealistic to expect the same efficacy. We want you to visit and explore these exotic lands and, throughout your exposure to different cultures, cultivate a sense of grace and patience when interacting with local merchants, shopkeepers, or service members who are accommodating you. Use the extra time waiting on your food constructively. Chat with your fellow bunkmates, journal, or simply marvel at where you find yourself in that moment. Allow yourself plenty of extra time between activities so you can avoid (as best as possible) that sense of urgency or stress that can creep in when running late.

Natasha

During my first group outing in Thailand we all sat down at a local restaurant and ordered the following: one pad thai, two red curries, one green curry, one papaya salad, two khoa pad (fried rice), and three tom yum goong (spicy shrimp soup). Ten very hungry backpackers from five different nations anxiously and excitedly awaited their feasts! Imagine our concern when the waitress approached the table with only three meals—two red and one green curry. The three people who'd been served followed social etiquette from their own cultures and did not touch their food while they waited patiently for everyone else's food to arrive. Approximately fifteen minutes later two fried rice made an appearance. At this point the initial meal recipients gave up and began eating. Anticipation and frustration grew as another ten minutes passed before the pad thai was served. Briefly after that the papaya salad and eventually the soup arrived. The last few frustrated and ravenous backpackers began to enjoy their food as the other plates were cleared.

One extremely upset gentleman in the group declared that he was going into that kitchen to complain! The gentleman returned with a look of guilt upon his face. He had learned that in the kitchen there was just the one woman, with the assistance of her child, preparing all of our meals. She only had one pan and one pot but was whizzing around the kitchen as fast as her legs would carry her. It was at that moment that we realized the level of respect we had for this woman running her restaurant alone to support her children. Even though she could not afford equipment, line cooks, prep cooks, and a server, she busted her ass and did what needed to be done.

PRO-TIP

In the spirit of keeping an even temper in most unpredictable situations and avoiding becoming hangry, always pack a snack!

- **Tipping & Paying the Bill**
Tipping may not seem like that big of a deal, but in many cultures tipping may be the employee's primary means of income as their base wage is well below the livable minimum. In other countries, tipping simply means rounding up to the next dollar. In others still, tipping can be considered insulting. Do not assume what you're used to is the social norm where you are traveling. In the spirit of being an enlightened traveler and respectful of those in the service industry, we highly advise that you take the time to check the local tipping customs. Remember, tipping may or may not extend to those outside the restaurant or bar industry. There are plenty of forums and websites that break down tipping by region quite specifically.

We also want to note it's not uncommon for novice backpackers to encounter social challenges when dining out in large, multicultural groups for the first time. This is most commonly caused by disagreement in tipping procedure, inability to read and decipher items on the bill, or not taking into account tax (if it is added at the end of the check) when putting in your portion of the money.

- **Understand the Local Tipping Customs** – Chat with the staff at your hostel or ask another traveler who has already been in the region a while. If you're comfortable, discuss what you learned prior to dining out with fellow travelers so you can be in agreement. While it might feel like nickel-and-diming to keep track of what you ordered so you don't overpay, this strategy can really help you stay on budget if traveling for a longer period of time. You can be benevolent and pick up the entire check or buy a round of drinks when you return home and are working again.

- **Separate Checks (let your server know before you order)** – If paying separately, inform the server when they first start to take your order (if they don't ask you first) to avoid confusion later. If paying separately is not an option, discuss how each person will be paying (card or cash) to be sure there is an accord. Remember that cash is king in most countries, so don't assume every place accepts credit or debit cards or that you can Venmo your portion. It may feel uncomfortable to broach this topic in advance, but rest assured it is even more uncomfortable when there is discord once the check arrives.

Natasha

As a very personal rule of thumb, I feel I am traveling with a quality group of people if all the money has been put forth for the bill and the final count is enough or too much compared to the total. If, once all the money toward the bill has been added and there is not enough to cover the total (including a culturally acceptable tip), I may reevaluate the company I am keeping. Again, this is a very personal feeling and is rooted in a deep understanding of the hospitality and service industry. Trust your own instincts!

DID YOU KNOW?

The Parthenon replaced an older temple of Athena, which historians call the Pre-Parthenon or Older Parthenon, that was demolished in the Persian invasion of 480 BC.

Navigating the Socials

A Cheat Sheet

- **Cultural Awareness**
Listen. Observe. Learn. Do your research; be prepared; pack a sarong, hat, and tissues; and be respectfully curious!

- **Drinking**
Drinking naturally lowers your inhibitions and makes you speak louder (and more freely about topics you might otherwise use hushed tones to communicate) and therefore makes it easier to become that gal. Don't be that gal!

- **Be Yourself**
Some cultures have a tarnished reputation in the traveling community for either being too loud, entitled, or disrespectful to alternative customs. Prove them all wrong by being your lovely, culturally respecting, and curious world-traveling self.

- **Social Media and Social Awareness**
Don't let moments happening IRL pass you by. Participate with the people you currently find yourself with on this planet and don't spend your time constantly posting or checking your Instagram, TikTok, Snapchat, or whatever hot new app will be invented in the next three weeks. On that note, don't bogart the shared computer at the hostel.

PRO-TIP
If you're not Canadian, don't put a maple leaf on your backpack in an attempt to disassociate from your home country and be internationally liked by all.

10 Bucket List Ideas

To check off your list

61. Eat a scorpion in Bangkok, Thailand ☐

62. WWOOF around the world ☐

63. Ride horses in Iceland ☐

64. Glimpse your reflection in the Salar de Uyuni, Bolivia ☐

65. Sail a freight ship from Scotland to Greenland ☐

66. Learn to make pasta from scratch in Rome ☐

67. Deepwater solo on Tonsai Beach, Thailand ☐

68. Bathe in a Turkish Hammam in Istanbul, Turkey ☐

69. Mark the beginning of Christmas at Las Posadas Celebration, Mexico ☐

70. Hang glide along the coast of Byron Bay, Australia ☐

199

8
FLINGS, BLING & ADVENTURES IN EATING

Date a girl who travels they said, but please, know that you will never tame her nor keep her. Because she'll never sign her letters off with a "your truly"—but always with a "see you when I see you"

—Lauren Klarfeld, How to keep a girl who travels...

The very first time you backpack alone for any extended length of time is nothing short of magical. The sincere naivety is nothing that can ever be recreated, no matter how many new countries you explore thereafter. The same can be said for each and every new relationship you experience on the road. Like a warm summer breeze or the heat coming off a roaring fire, they'll embrace you with their warmth and leave you feeling cool in their absence.

Many first-time travelers set out with a friend. We'll concede that traveling with someone you already know can provide a lot of comfort and security (at least initially) but believe us when we say it will limit your exposure and experiences. When you make the exciting and, let's face it, slightly scary decision to travel alone, you don't have a built-in support system to fall back on. Unless you intend on taking a vow of silence or celibacy (tried it, didn't stick), you will be required to put yourself out there, again and again, usually going first in smiles, greetings, questions, or invitations. Stepping outside of your comfort zone in this way will all but guarantee a full and complete social experience on the road like nothing else will. It's intimidating and scary as hell, but you'll be happy you did and even more badass (than you already are for deciding to travel in the first place) for being brave and outgoing.

Like Gabrielle Reece and Laird Hamilton explain in a 2017 interview with Tim Ferriss, we believe in going first. This is a philosophy we find applicable to what you're about to embark on in your travel experiences. Essentially, "going first" is the idea of showing up intentionally in your own life and others. This can be as simple as smiling at a stranger on the street or being the first to say hello to an employee in a shop or telling those you love in your life that they are appreciated without expecting anything in return. As Gabrielle puts it, "you have to go first because now we're being trained in this world, ➜

nobody's going first anymore." By going first while traveling, you will naturally open yourself up to opportunities otherwise un-extended to those who keep to themselves or who only stick with those they know.

It's not uncommon for those traveling together to keep to themselves and not become as engaged in meeting new people or deviating from a planned itinerary. It's less common that two or more traveling companions will branch off onto independent adventures and then meet back up again. When you're young and traveling to foreign countries for the first time, it's understandable that you'd want to be with someone you already know and trust. However, many friendships have been strained or altogether lost while traveling together internationally because, well, it's stressful! Therefore, trust us in our continued persistence of getting you on board with the idea of traveling alone, at least for your first few trips!

Kim

After my very first solo backpacking trip, I forevermore said that I would never marry anyone I hadn't traveled abroad with first. Believe it or not, you can hide a lot of crazy when you live with someone, even for a long period of time. When you're traveling however, you can't hide your coping mechanisms or stress-related idiosyncrasies that appear when your train has been delayed three hours, causing you to miss your connecting flight. Now you've got to find a place to stay in a seedy part of town and haven't eaten anything except an unbuttered baguette and a flat white six hours prior, so you're hangry as fuck because you'd planned to cook pasta at the hostel upon arrival. I'm just saying, traveling (especially on a budget) shows a person's true colors and they're not always pretty.

If you find someone you can harmoniously travel with even when shit hits the fan and all your plans fall apart, hold on tight (but not crazy lady tight) because that sort of connection is nothing short of magical. The travel relationships you forge don't have to result in marriage or even be sexual in nature. They don't even have to cross multiple borders, but when you meet someone you can explore a city, village, or the world with, especially if you just met on a train that afternoon, it's a dragon you're willing to chase for the rest of your life.

Love on the Road

Falling in love while traveling is uniquely special and will create lasting memories and legendary stories. With that said, heed our warning and take a few solo selfies without your newfound flame by the ancient temple for you to look back on years down the road, just in case it's not the long-lasting kind of love.

Meeting travelers on the road allows you to see a very special version of that person. Like you, they are currently experiencing their freest selves, sometimes for the very first or only time. There's a kindredness you can spot and subsequently relate to when you meet other travelers. The uniqueness of your experiences escalates attractions, allowing you to quickly enter (or altogether skip) the awkward, getting to know you or orchestrated meet-cute phase of a relationship. Afternoons are spent swimming in waterfalls while late nights are dedicated to dreaming of your next destination in a shared hammock under the stars. All the while the absence of reality blissfully resides in the distance, not getting in the way like it otherwise would, thereby allowing you to truly exist with this person who was put on this earth for you to share this moment with. We truly wish this special experience for everyone at some point in their travels!

As we will later discuss in detail, the road has a way of changing you, and the process of returning home changes you too. For some it's less obvious, perhaps their time abroad was just an opportunity to check off that "one crazy summer" bucket list item before career and family responsibilities took hold. For others, it's profoundly life altering, and every dollar earned moving forward is the next plane ticket to somewhere exotic. Regardless if it's intentional or simply a familiar routine, when most people return home, their old habits and patterns return to them.

For example:

Your bohemian Australian boyfriend with the free-spirited, peace-loving attitude who quit smoking because you hated it may very well light that first cigarette upon being welcomed home by the lads of his old rugby team and immediately become a judgmental drunk. We're just saying, it could happen.

Similarly, you can't predict how you'll change either upon returning home from a life-changing trip. We bring this up because it's entirely possible you'll meet someone (a friend or lover) that you may decide to visit during or after your trip and after they've also returned home. It's amazing to be invited by a worldly stranger that you connected with in such a unique way to their home and country. We only want to manage your expectations in ways neither of us were prepared for. There will be differences you'll inevitably notice in that individual when they're in their home hosting you, the continuing traveler. They likely have regained their sense of responsibility to work, family, friends, obligations, etc. whereas you may still be the carefree traveler they first met. It's possible a bit of the veneer might wear off during the course of your visit if you can't rekindle that same connection that drew you together when you were gallivanting abroad. It might only be years later—in hindsight and after a good amount of sadness in reflection—that understanding falls into place after those travel relationships naturally shift.

...but sometimes you find the one!

Natasha

Falling in love while traveling is an experience that I have found can't quite be replicated at home. Falling for a stranger from a foreign land in a foreign land is probably the closest embodiment of sheer romance. While there are outliers and very unromantic locales, I can assure you that most places lend themselves to quite a whirlwind of romantic experience. Everyone I have ever met traveling agrees the best romances are the ones that we know in our hearts will not extend past the current journey. Removing the pressure of the future and any everyday responsibilities does something to the psyche I can't quite explain that allows it to release all anxiety. When you combine that with the wind, sweat, and smells of an exotic locale and the feeling that around every corner you will find a new adventure, a new taste, and a new vista, it becomes intoxicating and alluring and brings out the best, most attractive, most daring, most exotic version of yourself (and others). All those impressions imprint onto the person you're with in that moment.

My most memorable experience of this kind of romance started on a journey between the northern border of Thailand and Laos. A friend and I found a travel organizer that specialized in helping backpackers cross from the northern Thai town of Chiang Mai to the Laos town of Luang Prabang via a two-day trip on the Mekong River. I first noticed him when we were about to embark on the journey. There was a little stall selling drinks and snacks for the journey. A very tall, handsome, blond German stood before me in line. We both took notice of each other via side-eyed stolen glances but said nothing. Later my stomach fluttered when I noticed he and his friend were grouped into our river boat.

The slow travel day wore on and boredom overtook any hesitation I might have held earlier about mingling, which was mirrored by those on board. A couple of Canadian guys who had been at our accommodations the night before offered each of us a beer from the case they had smuggled onto the boat. One beer led to multiple beers and friendships were easily established based on our Southeast Asian adventures. →

Fast forward to when we arrived back in Bangkok, and I found myself sitting in a hotel with the aforementioned handsome German; I tried to act cavalier with this newfound mate. Throughout the journey we had become quite close but had pretended our feelings were lighthearted and the attraction was mostly carnal. In that moment, sitting in that hotel, we both knew better. The hours until his flight became a weight on our hearts as we curled up together for what we both knew would be the last time. My throat hurt and exhaustion overcame me. I had become sick during our travels and needed to rest, but I refused to miss these last moments. When the alarm sounded, a reminder it was time for him to go, my eyes welled up as I hugged him goodbye. It was in that moment he bent down and whispered in my ear, "I fell in love with you", and with that parting whisper, he was gone.

Sex and the Hostel

"Years ago when I was backpacking through western Europe, I was just outside Barcelona hiking in the foothills of Mount Tibidabo..."

Friends, S8, E4: The One with the Videotape

Like all things related to backpacking, there is an etiquette to pursuing sexual relationships on the road. They won't all be with fellow travelers either. Some will be with a sexy local who finds you exotic and intoxicating. You may hit it off with someone you've met on a tour and didn't want your time together to end, so it didn't. Maybe you connect with a traveler with no plans and no itinerary, and you happen to be traveling in the same direction at the same time. What starts off as platonic develops into something sexual. All are possible scenarios, and all are worth exploring and experiencing!

Our hope is through each meet-cute you experience you'll file away instinctual information that will make the next relationship experience that much more memorable and socially considerate for your neighboring hostel bunkmates. We guarantee that with a little bit of false bravado (aka: fake it till you make it) and a whole lot of trusting of your instincts, you will fine tune your bullshit radar so that within the span of a handshake and a pint, you can determine if you want to travel with, shag, or say goodbye to the person you've just met on your journey. ➔

Speaking of shagging (having sex) hold your head high in knowing there's no walk of shame here. You are free to love and be loved as you traverse this planet. Just because you're traveling alone doesn't mean you need to be lonely. You do, however, need to be safe as well as courteous of your fellow hostel bunkmates. Hone your instincts and then trust them!

Unlike traditional hotels, hostels are each uniquely designed to allow travelers a more at-home or distinctly not-at-home experience, and within that you might find some secluded hideaway where you can enjoy a bit more privacy. Carrie Bradshaw may have had a lot to say about Sex in the City, but she never talked about sex in a hostel. If she had, she would certainly have revealed that bunk beds that have seen a lot of travelers over the years squeak no matter how quiet or careful you think you are being. For this reason, if you find yourself in a squeaky situation, the private showers can be your best friend.

As with all things, use your common sense and remember that if you think you're being super quiet at 3:00 a.m. when you are hammered and shagging on the bottom bunk of a shared twelve-bunk hostel room, we promise, you are not!

Condoms

For reasons personal to you, sex or intimacy while traveling may be the furthest thing from your list of priorities, and we fully support all of those choices, but we still highly recommend traveling with condoms. Buy them at home and bring them along for the trip, buy them in the airport, buy them in the bodega in Guatemala, steal them from your roommate for all we care (although we don't actually condone stealing), but always have condoms in your pack or available to you.

No matter how well you think you know yourself or how pure your intentions may be, international backpacking has a way of presenting alluring people along your path and outright changing you. Simply put, it's always better to be prepared and have condoms (and not use them) than to find yourself without them and in need of one.

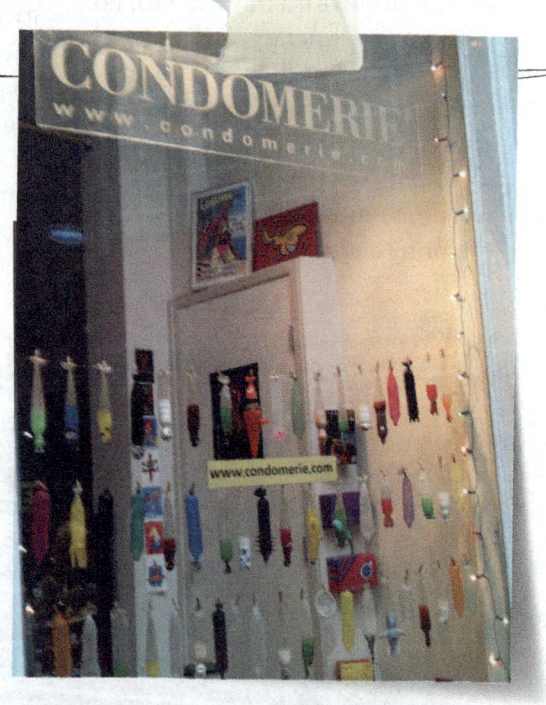

Breaking Up on the Road

We'll keep this one short. If you form a bond with someone and it has run its course, be considerate how you end things. Take care not to tarnish the wonderful memories you shared. While you may meet those married couples who claim to have met while traveling when single, they are few and far between. It's far more likely the relationships you develop will be singularly tied to the experience of where you find yourself in the world and, because of that, you also never know when you'll run into that person again. Trust our experience: the world is a very small place when living that backpacker lifestyle.

Traveling with Another Traveler (Platonically)

Sometimes you meet someone that you just gel with. It's effortless, as if you've known them your entire life and you don't waste a lot of time questioning if you should travel alone with this person. These encounters are truly kismet, and if you don't try and control the outcome too much, can lead you on some of the grandest, most memorable adventures you'll ever experience. While they don't come around often, when they do, you'll know it. You'll meet in the most random ways like on a train, folding laundry at your hostel, or on a weekend tour. The opportunities to meet are endless.

Take advantage of these moments and don't think too much about the nature of your relationship. Maybe you'll remain platonic or maybe you will explore some sexual chemistry. Regardless, let it happen and enjoy it for the gift that it is. These will be the people you look back on year after year and wonder where life's adventures have taken them, if they're happy, and what they are doing now. You may lose and regain touch over and over as the years span out, and that's okay too. With social media, it's easier to keep tabs on the ones who touch your heart. There's nothing quite like rekindling a lost connection with someone you randomly met on a train and traversed this planet with.

Kim

One summer, on a train bound for Munich, Germany, I met the funniest, most kindhearted Australian backpacker. Earlier, I'd spent the afternoon exploring Neuschwanstein Castle with a Kiwi bloke (guy), whom I would later visit in his home country of New Zealand on two separate occasions. In arriving in Munich, the three of us plus two American girls found ourselves drinking oversized steins at Hirschgarten, the largest Biergarten in Munich. After several steins and a bellyful of laughs, the Australian and I decided we would like to travel together for a while and see where the journey took us. There was no set itinerary, no plan of action, no timetable to adhere to, and that suited me just fine.

What started out as a random introduction on a train turned into exploring Germany, Austria, Switzerland, Italy, Sweden, and Norway with someone who felt like my very best friend despite only knowing him for one month. While our relationship wasn't sexual in nature, I felt more deeply attracted and attuned to him than anyone else I ever met. I lamented for years after that our relationship didn't amount to anything physical.

Our friendship changed after I visited him in Australia the following January. He was the first traveler I'd connected with so deeply that I flew to the other side of the world just to see him again (and be his date for his father's wedding). But I was young and still naive to what the dynamic of visiting a traveler once they had returned home would entail. I didn't yet possess the understanding that we were in two completely different headspaces and points in life, and it ultimately changed the dynamic of what we were to each other and the interactions we would have.

Though he showed me an amazing time and was the most wonderful of hosts and tour guides, it became apparent that our time in Australia marked the end of what we had been to each other in Europe. I regret not being able to understand that reality more clearly at the time. While I had returned home briefly after backpacking Europe to finish college, I hadn't taken the time to settle into much of a routine. Instead, my time at home was focused on finishing college with the express intent of getting back on the road the moment I graduated college. In fact, I left to visit him in Australia and embark on my yearlong voyage around the world only one week after I graduated.

I never traveled with anyone in quite the same way ever again even though I met many wonderful travelers heading in the same direction for periods of time. Exploring Europe with that person was nothing short of life changing for my first time traveling alone. Years later, we were able to reconnect briefly, but I'm not sure he truly knows just how special he was and remains to me. I continue to miss him and our bellyfuls of laughs.

Valuables & Bling

You're going to have enough to worry about throughout your travels (like locating your hostel, keeping on budget, and navigating your way between towns or countries, just to name a few) without being constantly worried about protecting valuable shit. Our advice, leave it at home!

For those items you simply can't travel without, for both men and women, always keep a small day pack, purse, or travel belt with you and try not to part with it for any reason!

- Need to put your pack on the roof of the van or the back of the bus?
Keep your day pack/purse/travel belt with you! ✓
- Need to run into a small shop and your larger pack is too big to come inside?
Your day pack/purse/travel belt can come with you. Never in any circumstance let your small pack out of your sight. ✓
- Taking an impromptu swim, kayak, or boat excursion?
Take inventory of your surroundings. Be sure to keep your stuff in sight. Better yet, put it in a waterproof bag and take it with you! ✓

Only if your hostel has a private safe or locker secured with your own personal lock or private combination do we recommend not carrying your valuable documents and cash with you. *Even then, we still suggest caution.*

Keep These Safe

- Passport
- International Driver's Permit (valid for 150 countries and can be obtained through AAA) – Handy if you want to rent a motorbike in Southeast Asia or an ATV to explore the Adriatic Islands
- Visas
- Vaccine and Immunization Documents
- Rail Pass (or other travel vouchers)
- ISIC/ISE/IYEC (if applicable)
- Money (cash, credit/debit cards, traveler's checks)
- Medicines (you may need a mini-backpack or fanny pack in this case)
- Food Allergy Card (if applicable)
- Phone (if necessary)
- Combination Lock (avoid locks that require keys that can get lost or be picked)

Leave These Home

- Jewelry (a simple gold or silicone band and basic watch is enough)
- Electronics (we covered this in detail previously)
- Multiple Credit Cards (one backup card is sufficient)
- Anything you'd be sad to lose or can't be replaced

A Note About Money

As a rule, don't carry too much cash on hand. While you should always have some currency on you (at least US$100 worth), it's not worth carrying so much that if you got robbed, you'd be left destitute. Lock some up in your hostel safe or locker and only go out with a limited amount when exploring new cities (which will also help keep you on budget). When you are traveling between locations, keep all your cash tucked safely inside your money belt (down your pants). If you keep it all in your pack or purse and that gets stolen, you'll be shit out of luck and we just don't want that for you!

The more you care about an item, the more likely you are doomed to lose it on the road. We can't explain this phenomenon but have seen (and experienced) it time and again. All this said, if you lose something important (not your passport, however), exhale and remember that it's just stuff. The region will usually sell items you need to replace.

Credit Card vs. Debit Card

While the use of credit/debit cards for everyday purchases are commonplace in the western world, there are still many countries that operate with cash economies. Debit cards are important when traveling to countries with cash economies; they provide protection from the risk of carrying excess cash, while still leaving the option to access local currencies as needed at ATMs. Just be sure to keep in mind that many foreign ATMs charge fees to access money from non-affiliated banks. Occasionally you will find banks that offer fee reimbursement, so it's a good idea to shop around to find the most travel-friendly bank account.

If you are traveling in a more advanced economy, credit cards can be a safer option than debit cards, especially if they get stolen.

Many credit cards have travel protection plans that you should investigate prior to leaving your home country. Even if you prefer American Express for purchases at home, opt for Visa or MasterCard while traveling internationally, which are still most widely accepted globally. If possible, request two card copies from your bank and keep them separately stored between your belongings.

The most ideal option is simply having one debit and one credit card (with hard copies stored separately or digitally). Keep one in your large pack and one in your day pack or purse. Use one when out exploring and leave the other securely stored in the hostel locker or safe. If one of your bags goes missing you can contact the bank, close the card, and transfer all your money to the safe account. Keep your passport with one of your cards and your driver's license (or any other form of identification) with the other.

Before you travel, call your bank and your credit card companies and tell them that you plan to travel. They have specific questions they'll ask including duration and which countries specifically you intend to travel through. It's okay if you don't have all the logistics mapped out yet, but

PRO-TIP
★ ★ ★ ★ ★

Not every hostel or town will give you the warm fuzzies or kumbaya sort of vibes. In these situations (where you literally just need a cheap, warm, safe bed for one night) we recommend sleeping with your money/travel belt on you, under your pajamas for safe keeping.

Be prepared to answer the following questions:

- ✳ When you'll be traveling
  (they may ask for exact dates)
- ✳ Where you'll be traveling
  (include regions or all countries you think you might travel to)
- ✳ How long you'll be traveling
  (a week, months, a year or more)

having a note on your account will lessen the likelihood of having your credit card frozen while abroad. While it may seem like a lot of hoops to jump through to use your credit card while traveling, we prefer them to debit cards. If your debit card becomes compromised, your entire account can be depleted, whereas credit cards have fraud protection and safety systems in place to safeguard your purchases and funds.

Debit cards are great for staying on a budget and traveling within your means; however, they are riskier if one should become compromised or stolen. If you plan to travel with a debit card, have two linked checking accounts back home and split your money between those two accounts in case you lose your debit card (store the two cards separately—one in your pack and one on your person). This way you can rest easy knowing all your funds won't be completely wiped out. If you opt to use your debit card to help keep you on your shoestring budget, consider writing your daily purchases, large and small, in your journal so you can visually manage where you are spending your monies.

At the end of the day, you want to know that if your backpack or purse gets stolen or lost, you will still be fine because you have your passport, money, and important documents or medicines on you always.

Reminder:
Taking cash advances out from credit cards can carry heavy interest rates, leading to unintended debt. We suggest this option only be used in case of emergency.

Adventures in Eating (and Drinking)

Chances are, if you're planning to travel for a while or are trying to budget on a shoestring, you'll probably eat a lot of peanut butter and pasta at your hostel with the other backpackers you meet. However, outside of the United States, it's quite common to come across inexpensive, seasonal, and delicious street food that might not always be found on a street! Toss out the notion that all meals must be enjoyed seated at a table. Sometimes train and bus stations will have quick grab-and-go options, as well as stand-alone carts, bodegas, and corner shops. For not much more than a loaf of bread, you can enjoy exquisite options that will delight your senses and not break the bank.

Blogs, apps, social media, and food-centric online streaming services make it easy to explore culinary cuisines from around the world from the comfort of your home. If you haven't figured it out by now, we want you to step out of your comfort zone and taste the world for yourself! One of the easiest and most authentic ways to explore any country is through its local culinary scene. No one is suggesting you eat dead bugs (but don't knock them till you try them!) or bite the tentacle off an octopus (actually, please don't do this one), but you don't have to be totally off the grid to experience exotic options. We just want you to be open to new ideas because it's super easy to say you don't like something without ever really giving it a try (as long as there are no food allergy concerns).

Many countries have food markets where you can shop for spices or ingredients for meals made back at your hostel, or you can try exotic fruits, veggies, or dishes directly from a farmer, chef, or stall cart. Often these dishes are regionally specific and perfectly in season. Unlike in the United States and other Western countries where you can buy produce year-round, regardless if it's being sold during its optimal growing season (for best flavor and ripeness), most countries only eat what's in season or has been caught, foraged, or butchered that day.

Because of this, and smaller refrigeration capacities in most private residences, it's not uncommon for people to shop daily for their meal ingredients. Additionally, those of you who suffer from food intolerances, sensitivities, or have outright allergies may find that you are able to eat foods you couldn't enjoy at home while traveling abroad.

Kim

Natasha and I have a mutual friend from the United States who has a very sensitive gluten intolerance and avoids all products and ingredients that could trigger a flare up, including all her favorite pastas and most baked goods. While in Italy on her honeymoon, she risked enjoying fresh, local pasta and came to realize she could not only tolerate it gastronomically but fully enjoyed her meals without the panic and stress of stomach discomfort. As a bonus, she is also now able to source that type of flour in the United States so she can bake and prepare fresh pasta anytime she wants!

ERIN
ALLERGIES
GLUTEN | DAIRY | SOY | EGG | RAW CRUCIFEROUS
NOT CELIAC

We don't take food allergies lightly, but still urge you—where you feel comfortable—to try the local options. Consider creating and traveling with a food allergy card (see left). You can have one tailored to your home language for when dining locally or custom-made to accommodate the language of the country you'll be traveling through.

Food Allergy Business Card

Neither of us suffer from food allergies or intolerances but a friend of Kim's who has severe food allergies suggests the following. Before you leave home create a two-sided food allergy business card in both English and the language of the country you'll be visiting. If you're traveling between regions, create it in a few in different languages. Laminate one copy and keep it safe in your travel belt. Include all your allergies. You can also learn to pronounce the words and practice your foreign language skills.

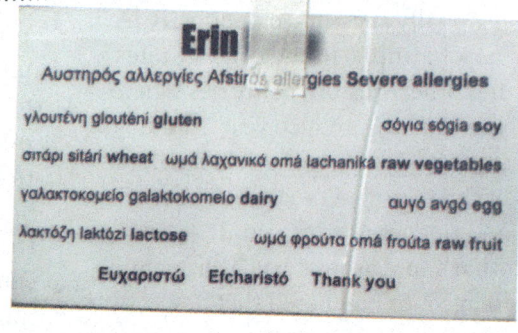

Bring extra cards with you. Feel free to give it to your waiter for the duration of the meal, allowing them to share it with the chef, which is especially useful if you're dining in a small, family operated establishment or street cart. If you leave it behind after a couple glasses of wine, no big deal, you've got extras!

Look online for companies that offer card printing services, many of which are economical for your needs and often run a savings special. Having this card available and ready to hand to your server is not only great for when you're traveling abroad but simplifies your dining restrictions when you're eating out at home too!

Water, Water Everywhere – Do You Dare to Drink?

When traveling through most of western Europe, the Americas, or Australasia, it's customary when dining at restaurants for the server to ask if you'd like sparkling water or still. Take note, in most cases, this is for an additional charge, and it's perfectly acceptable (and safe) to ask for tap water instead, which is free of charge.

If you decide to travel through more remote areas, you might be cautioned (by your guidebook, a trusted travel blog, a friend who also explored that region, or even your server while in said country) not to drink the local water.

If consuming local water is of genuine concern (because certain bacteria are very disagreeable with Western bowels), look for ways to mitigate exposure. There are water purifying tablets, portable filtration straws (great for camping) and, of course, bottled water (though, from a sustainability standpoint, this is not our first choice). While it's manageable to drink only bottled water (though not budget- or eco-friendly), one thing to be aware of is you can't control how produce is washed and drinks or meals are prepared. For that matter, it's also easy to forget to use bottled water when brushing your teeth, which can lead to an unexpected bout of dietary distress if you're not paying attention.

Kim

I experienced this firsthand in Mongolia after contracting a severe case of dysentery that resulted in several weeks of stomach and bowel distress even after returning home.

Common bacterial digestive disorders from contaminated food or water include:

- Dysentery
- Cholera
- Typhoid

When it comes to traveler's diarrhea (it's a thing) and dehydration, rest and self-care are often the first line of defense. We'll leave you with the following belly-sensitive checklist to consider before heading on your next adventure:

- **Loperamide tablets** – trust us, they come in handy!
- **Electrolyte packets** – these can be mixed into your water bottle and are good for a hot day's hike or aiding in hangovers.
- **Avoid fruits and vegetables with edible skins** – while more effective at rehydrating you than water due to natural electrolytes, you'll want to avoid fruits and vegetables with skins that can't peel off or break apart. Stick to fruits like oranges, pineapple, avocados, or pomegranates where the inside isn't contaminated by pesticides, water, or bacteria.

10
Bucket List Ideas
To check off your list

71. Marvel at the culture and natural rainbow colors of Hormuz Island, Iran ....
72. Explore Gorham's Cave Complex, an UNESCO World Heritage Site in Gibraltar ....
73. Ride the Gelmer Funicular in Bern, Switzerland ....
74. Flutter in the monarch butterfly biosphere in Michoacán, Mexico ....
75. Dive in the world's deepest pool in Dubai ....
76. Cruise along the shoreline in Mykonos, Greece ....
77. Take a safari in Zambia's South Luangwa National Park ....
78. Sleep in a panoramic glass neo tepee just two hours outside of Moscow, Russia ....
79. Learn to surf in Tamarindo, Costa Rica ....
80. Hug the world's tallest trees in Sequoia National Park, California, USA ....

221

9
THE SOLITUDE IN DREAMING DIFFERENTLY

Karen, her elbows folded on the deck-rail, wanted to share with someone her pleasure in being alone: this is the paradox of any happy solitude.
—Elizabeth Bowen, The House in Paris

It's inevitable, if you spend any length of time traveling alone, that you'll run into stressors of required consideration and roadblocks of loneliness. You'll inevitably become homesick. This could be for your family, friends, a specific food or establishment, or even a ritual or routine. You'll lament the comforts of familiarity even while living out your greatest dream or adventure. You'll reach this point of longing, whether it's witnessing (yet another) beautiful sunset, beholding the spectacular countryside while traveling to your next destination on a train, or amid a group of travelers while wishing someone familiar were there to share the experience with you.

Loneliness happens, and when it does, it's good to remind yourself that while you might be feeling lonely, you are not alone. While your first trip alone will undoubtedly be fully engaging, it may not be until your second, third, or thirteenth expedition that the weight of loneliness might rear its heavy head. When that inevitably sets in, try to remember that these moments of longing and quiet introspection are vital to appreciating the external jubilation that occurs in moments of adventure or astonishment.

Possibly the most important item you'll want to pack, besides your passport, is a travel journal. Even if you blog or send personal email updates to family and friends back home, journaling is a private and constant companion when you're feeling the most alone or isolated. While you're going to experience events you want to share openly, there will be others you wish to keep private. Even if you're not a writer, look at it as a time capsule so you can revisit those moments in the future when you're at a crossroads, questioning the next big thing, and need a reminder of how brave and amazing you (still) are. ➜

No one is asking you to pen the great American novel. Your journal could literally be a series of doodles or bullet point observations including all the countries and towns in between. Journaling is a powerful way to empty your mind of all the emotions that bubble up when traveling abroad while also becoming a physical talisman reminding you of the great fortune you've experienced in having traveled. It is possible to be happy and sad and confident and insecure throughout this process. Having an intensely personal, firsthand account to later reflect on will be invaluable to your present and future self.

Consider the financial and life decisions you must make every day while traveling. These can directly impact your health, happiness, safety, and financial security—especially when traveling for extended periods of time.

Some of the most basic considerations are:

1 Where will you sleep tonight?
- Hostel
- Hotel
- Couch surf
- Camp
- Park bench

2 How much cash do you have left?
- Did you set a daily allowance?
- Are you in an expensive city or an inexpensive country?
- What's the currency conversion like and how far will your funds stretch?

3 Is it safe?
- Is the hostel you can afford on the sketchy side of town sandwiched between an XXX store and a bail bond office or are you just going to pull off at the next beach overlook and pitch your tent? Both options may present themselves-sometimes within the same week of traveling!

4 How will you get there?
- What is your mode of transportation today?
- Does your budget afford you the convenience of public transit or will you need to walk everywhere?
- Once you arrive, assuming you didn't time it well, will you be locked out for cleaning?
- Where will you store your stuff? Assuming everything you possess is on your back, it has value and must be protected.

5 What will you eat?
- Do you have the budget to eat out or do you need to find a grocery store and cook in?
- Do you have access to a kitchen or a portable camp stove?
- How will you preserve or store your leftovers?

Citizens of Commonwealth countries might be able to pick up the odd job along the way to replenish or sustain their finances, but US citizens are often limited to under the table sorts of gigs or free labor in exchange for a reduced rate or altogether free accommodation.

For backpackers, this typically involves cleaning bathrooms, kitchens, turning beds, and doing laundry at a hostel. This is a great option in peak season but isn't always an option in the off season and can alter the timeline of your day of adventuring. Should you decide to seek this type of exchange, remember a business owner is offering you a job (regardless of if it's for two hours or two weeks) and it should be done well and with future travelers' interests in mind.

The Mindfuck of Long-Term Travel

Traveling for long periods of time will change you. Your reality may seem unimaginable to everyone back home, but the people you'll encounter along the way totally understand and relate. It's such a small subset of humans that truly have the guts, fortitude, and wherewithal to follow through on their dreams of world travel. Because of this, you may find yourself frustrated in trying to articulate your daily life, especially when it switches gears from bucket list vacation to world traveler. While most everyone following your adventures back home are super stoked for you, it's inevitable you'll start to hear whispers or rumblings from friends and less immediate family members inquiring when are you coming home and getting a real job? You can't just travel the world forever.

If you're gone long enough, you're bound to receive a backhanded compliment or two about your adventures. Try not to take these comments to heart. Remind yourself that you're doing something most people only dream of, and they are likely jealous of your freedom at this moment in time. This is a difficult request but try not to internalize guilt from these comments (which may be easier said than done, in truth). While these moments will inevitably be present with any extended length of travel, it's important not to let them hinder or suppress your spirit of adventure. Most people don't follow through on their dreams, not because they don't have the money or can't make the time, but because they're scared. Fear can be motivating or debilitating and will also keep you vigilant when navigating the unknown alone. We wouldn't trade even one moment of sadness or isolation along the way in exchange for not having gone in the first place. →

Conversely, sometimes it is about longing and the comfort of someone who knows you intimately. Whether deciding to travel without a romantic partner or ending a relationship in order to pursue a dream of traveling, knowing you need to go it alone can really mess with your mind, never mind your heart. This said, we all know when we should or shouldn't be in certain relationships. We are not here to solicit love advice, only to say we understand that stepping out of these relationships isn't always easy, and sometimes we allow them to go on for much longer than they reasonably should at a personal sacrifice to both parties involved. If the pull of global adventure draws you, don't let anything or any person stand in the way of realizing your dreams. Those who truly love you will let you go. Trust us both—you may find your way back to that person in the future, and you'll both be that much more alluring and interesting for the independence you embraced.

Kim

July hit me like a sledgehammer filled with loneliness. Just six months into a one-year trip around the world and coming off the high of vagabonding my way alone through Australia and New Zealand, I found myself back in the UK, nursing my third glass of wine while crying in the narrow stairwell of my friend's home. I was missing my on-again, off-again boyfriend (who was currently stationed in Guam), wondering what in the actual fuck I was doing with my life and whether I made the wrong choice in deciding to chase this now full-blown addiction I had to travel.

The previous July, I had been halfway through my first solo European adventure, having the time of my life, chalking it all up as a once-in-a-lifetime experience, and living everyday like it was my last. It felt possessive and fleeting and magical. I didn't want my adventures to end and had made solid arguments to my family back home as to why I wouldn't be returning to finish my college degree. I'd been offered an apartment to rent for US$100 per month in Vernazza, Italy, literally spitting distance from the Mediterranean! I mean, would you want to return home to finish college?

In the end reason, sensibility, and (let's face it) familial guilt won out, and I returned home to complete my final semester. My consolation in returning home was knowing I had saved a ton of cash by cleaning hostels and would have enough money leftover to book an outbound flight the moment my graduation was official. Don't get me wrong, I had a wonderful home to return to. I had friends that I cared for, a high school sweetheart, and a job if I wanted it. I wasn't trying to escape reality or avoid responsibility, instead I was searching for something that only ever felt like it came into focus when I was navigating the unknown. This was and remains difficult to explain to those that don't get it.

And so, one week after my final senior class (I skipped the graduation formalities), with US$1,000 saved and an Around the World plane ticket secured, I boarded a plane and began my yearlong adventure, once again alone. I reunited with friends I'd met the summer prior and met new ones along the way. I slowed down to speed up and tried to remember that this time it wasn't a sprint, it was a marathon. →

For the first six months, I indulged in every possible way, and it was starting to take its toll. My health was far from optimal, my travel relationships (both friendships and flings) were intense but short-lived, and though I was having the time of my life, it was difficult to articulate the full spectrum of precious moments to my loved ones back home anxiously awaiting my updates. Though they wanted to, they simply couldn't understand my range of high and low emotions because they weren't there experiencing the day-to-day with me. I found myself privately journaling my emotions and publicly emailing my experiences in the absence of being able to share them with someone who intimately knew me. It felt isolating and disjointed.

On top of that, I felt guilty that I was here, and my friends and family were there. I had tried to convince friends back home to travel with me, but no one felt like they could commit for one reason or another (you've probably heard a few of those excuses yourself). Now, friends who had once been excited to receive my updates slowly stopped checking in or replying.

As the months went on, even though I set out alone, I found myself feeling more (emotionally) isolated. While my parents were my biggest cheerleaders, there were few friends back home who understood why I would volunteer to scrub toilets, clean kitchens, and make beds in exchange for just one more day on this assumed "vacation." They, after all, were living in reality and had real hardships and responsibilities to contend with. My tears of loneliness were not based in reality and did not warrant offering me a tissue.

Making the leap from short-term tourist to long-term traveler is a weird thing. No one seems to explain with any real clarity that eventually it stops being this epic adventure (though adventurous events do happen) and simply starts being life, and while it may not currently resemble the life your friends and family are living back in the real world, it's your reality and in many ways is a return to primal needs: food, water, shelter. Anything extra is a bonus that you'll be all that more stoked to experience. My point is, when you're on the road for a long time, despite what your curated social media feed might reflect or your emails might say, at some point the veneer wears off and it stops being a vacation and starts becoming your new normal.

I can only speak from personal experience, but all those aforementioned points to consider take a toll, one I always found worth paying, but expensive, nonetheless. I refer to expense not financially but in committing to leave the safety and comforts of what you know back home — family, friends, culture, and security — to journey on a mission of education and self-discovery or, as I referred to that year, "grad school." This was not a gap year between college and the start of my career, this was an extension of my education to further define my cultural understanding and life experiences and see if there was a new normal outside of what those back home defined "normal" to be.

Distance and time are fickle definitions in the subculture of backpacking. In the eyes of the world, an American traveling for up to two weeks (an extensive length of time by US standards) is considered unusual because it typically requires a flexible job or generous employer. For Europeans, two weeks is an expected annual holiday not to be confused with a longer sabbatical that is rarely afforded to Americans. →

...a star that can still be seen in a city skyline

In the beginning, my decision to travel made everyone around me proud. As a blue-eyed, blond-haired, single, white, American woman traveling alone around Europe for three months armed with only a backpack, passport, and rail pass with no planned itinerary in my early twenties, I was brave and to be commended. A once-in-a-lifetime opportunity! Hoorah! However, to immediately set out again and put into action an unplanned, unguided, adventure-seeking, education expanding, culture confronting year of exploration and self-discovery was crazy to most, and downright irresponsible to many. It was interesting to see how choices I was making for myself created turmoil in others (kind of like being a vegan).

Jealousy rears its head in interesting ways, and it's important to identify that you might not always receive the feedback you're expecting when trying to share your travel experiences or convey your concerns. It took a long time to recognize and accept that travel changed me, because in my eyes, I was just l-i-v-i-n'. If you set out on the road less traveled, you will change. It would be sad if you didn't. So be brave. Be irreverent. Evolve.

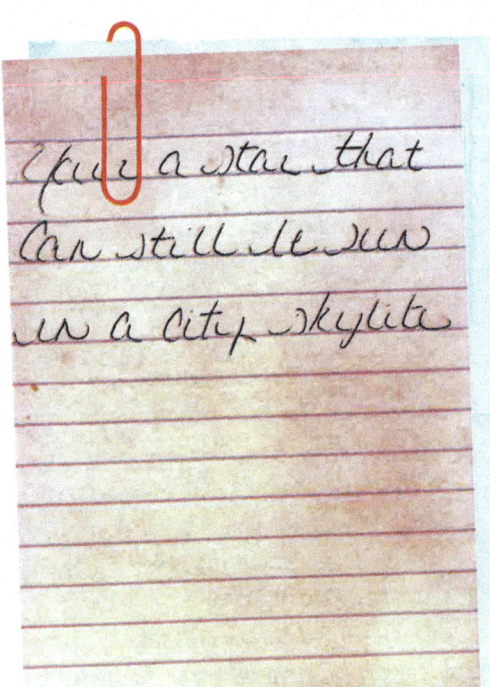

In the backpacker culture, Americans rarely cross over from being the proverbial short-term tourist into long-term traveler, which is usually reserved (almost exclusively) for Aussies, Kiwis, and South Africans. Perhaps it's how we're conditioned as Americans growing up, but I've become increasingly aware of a certain guilt that sets in whenever embarking on anything outside the confines of societal norms and a further frustration in not being able to articulate to anyone who hasn't themselves turned their back on the status quo and blazed their own travel trail.

What we're simply trying to convey is the sooner you can accept that some of your relationships back home might change, should you accept the challenge of exploring this badass blue planet, the easier it will be to navigate the inevitable solitude and introspection that you will experience even when you're surrounded by people. It's hard to explain. In a lot of ways, it sucks. We'd be lying if we said it was as sexy, glossy, and curated as social media would have those back home believe. It's not anything you can prepare for because it's tied to this beautiful understanding that what you have experienced is so profoundly defining that you'll want to shout from the rooftop with happiness and share it with anyone that will listen.

The unfortunate truth is those who have never done what you've set out (or are about) to do just simply can't understand the mindset life will find you in or how it will ultimately change your thinking. They might really want to and are happy you're happy, but if the travel bug bites you and you continue down its path, eventually your friends back home may become less enthusiastic in replying to your updates. Life gets in the way and how you choose to live yours isn't any better or worse than your friend who graduated, got a job, and started a family at twenty-three years old. For all the ways you can't relate to them, neither can they to you.

The good news is there are those who will get it! You will find yourself years down the road having just met a kindred spirit in one of those wacky, like-attracts-like sorts of ways and you'll share a pint, and one story will run into the next story and you'll simply want to jump out of your skin with excitement almost as if you're reliving your memories in real time. It will happen, and when it does, it will be glorious. It just doesn't happen that often, but it's all the sweeter for it to happen at all.

10 Bucket List Ideas

To check off your list

81. Float a bamboo raft in Jamaica .... ☐
82. Bathe in thermal baths in the ancient city of Saturnia, Italy ...... ☐
83. Hike Rainbow Mountain in Peru .... ☐
84. Marvel at the Puga Valley in Ladakh, India .... ☐
85. Take a vertical ride up a desert dune in Dubai .... ☐
86. Learn how to kite surf in Cumbuco, Brazil .... ☐
87. Take an ecotour in New South Wales, Australia .... ☐
88. Conquer your fear of heights on the
    Mount Huashan Plank Trail in China .... ☐
89. Watch elephants play in Amboseli National Park, Kenya .... ☐
90. Mountain bike in Chamonix, France .... ☐

233

10

YOUR EVOLUTION AND WHY YOU SHOULDN'T WAIT TO GO

If you want to hold this feeling in your hands, you will have to dig for it yourself. There is no other way, no shortcut, no online course, no magic recipe.

—Toby Israel, Vagabondess: *A Guide to Solo Female Travel*

Natasha – Reflections on Why Soon Might Not Be Soon Enough

In 2021 I revisited Puerto Rico. After having a spectacular time on my original trip in 2010, I made a list of all my previous favorite places with the intent to return with my fiancé. At the top of my list was kayaking in the Bioluminescent Mosquito Bay of Vieques. For years I proclaimed that this was one of the highlights of my travels and couldn't wait to share the experience with someone I love. I booked the flights, Airbnb, and rental car. →

I reserved the kayaks and planned the route. I excitedly riled up expectations of what an incredible experience we were about to have together. I couldn't wait to show him how beautiful the world could really be.

Cut to sheer devastation. What I had considered one of the most spectacular sights on earth was simply gone. The waters that once radiated light when touched, much "like a glow stick at night" had grown dim. The tour guides, desperate to still capitalize on this dying attraction, distributed a tarp to spread across the twenty kayaks so that we could get a brief glimpse of what was left of the glow. To say that I was overwhelmed with grief would be an understatement. The most magical experience of my life was not one that could be shared with anyone ever again. It was simply gone. Upon our return to the Airbnb, I rummaged through articles on the internet to find out what happened (in hopes that it was just a seasonal fluke) only to find a New York Times article entitled "Puerto Rico Debates Who Put Out the Lights in Mosquito Bay" which tried (and failed) to explain "why, suddenly and inexplicably, one of the world's most famous bioluminescent bays had dimmed."

It dawned on me, not for the first time, how fast the world changes and how much of what I have already seen may no longer exist for the traveler after me. Old Freak Street, one of my favorite streets to wander in Kathmandu, Nepal, had been devastated by a 2015 earthquake. "In the Tubing", a well-known and wildly fun backpacker destination in Vang Vieng, Laos, had been shut down (rightfully) after the deaths of several backpackers. What I wouldn't give to have a few extra moments back in those locales. What I wouldn't give for you to be able to visit and experience what I have experienced.

We are not the first generation to see the demise of a travel mecca. Thousands of vagabonds journeyed overland on "the hippie trail" between Europe and South Asia, mainly through Iran, Afghanistan, Pakistan, India, and Nepal in the 1950s through the 1970s. There is no shortage of travel memoirs and tales waxing lyrically on the old glories of the trail. Unfortunately, the Iranian Revolution and Soviet invasion of Afghanistan led to permanent closure of the route.

In an essay written in 1980, famous travel writer Bruce Chatwin laments the Afghanistan of his youth, sharing "...that will not bring back the things we loved...We shall not lie on our backs at the Red Castle and watch the vultures wheeling over the valley where they killed Ghengis. We will not read Babur's memoirs in his garden at Istalif and see the blind man smelling his way around the rose bushes." He continues, "We will not stand on the Buddha's head at Bamiyan, upright in his niche like a whale in a dry dock...Nor shall we get back the smell of the bean fields; the sweet, resinous smell of deodar wood burning, or the whiff of a snow leopard at 14,000 feet. Never, Never. Never."

However depressing, we are not stressing these tales with the intention of demoralizing you about what you have missed, but to encourage you to get out and see the things you have always dreamed of seeing, because nothing in this world is guaranteed to last forever. →

The wonders that await you the first time you travel alone are like nothing in this world and can never be recreated. The fact they can never be re-experienced is a good thing because it will leave you spellbound and chasing the dragon of undiscovered alchemy for years to come. For those courageous few it is revolutionary in its ability to change your entire perspective and personal narrative. Not only in how you view others but in how you come to understand the capabilities you possess. It's easy to forget those lessons though. It's easy to return home, get caught back up in the everyday patterns and lose sight of the strength and freedom that is born in traveling alone.

Don't get us wrong, traveling with a friend or partner can be awesome, and eventually you may find yourself in a relationship with someone who loves to travel as much as you. Congratulations if that's you! However, in all healthy relationships there is a need for space—space that's given freely and space that is requested. It's within this distance that you remain interesting, loyal, and true to yourself. If your heart is promised first to the mistress that is travel and second to your partner, then you may have difficult conversations in your future. Especially if they love to travel too.

Kim

Speaking from experience, my husband loves to travel as much as I do. He has supported nearly every harebrained scheme or goal I've ever set for myself. He has listened to endless drafts of chapters, prologues, and letters to you, knowing that the reminiscing makes me pine to cash in some savings and take a solo journey, something I haven't done in several years now. Together, we've been around the world, and I've loved every adventure I've ever taken with him. It's a glue that binds us, and I always remind him that (I feel) I'm the best version of myself when we're braving the unknown. And yet, even he finds it difficult to understand why I would still want to take a trip alone, without him. This is compounded by the fact that I do not dream small and those remaining places at the top of my bucket list are places he would be open to exploring as well.

I wish I had an explanation that might satisfy him, but at the end of the day, it's like tapping into a power source that ignites my entire being and makes me the very best version of myself. Even now, I can't quite find the words. The desire to venture out alone and remind myself that I'm (still) capable of anything feels woven into my DNA, which in a way was rewritten at the age of twenty-two.

The need to get back on the road beckons the seasoned traveler like smoldering embers, ready to reignite. Simply put, travel changes you. It may not be immediate or even outwardly obvious, but one day you'll realize that you're different. You'll find yourself recounting years not by birthdays or milestones of career achievement but rather countries explored, revisited, or anticipated.

Some years you'll visit one country, other years you touch soil in more than fourteen. You'll feel restless and unfocused until you sort out your next trip. Some people travel to escape, others travel to discover. Going home has its own merits. The transition from non-traveler to traveler and then back again results in a perspective you did not previously possess. Unlike going to college or straight into the workforce, traveling teaches you more about your personal value system and helps to better hone your communication and reasoning skills than anything either of us have done before or experienced since. You can't learn about the world or yourself from a book.

Returning home is part of the process. Whether returning home is anticipated or dreaded, it's vital to the overall experience. You can't enjoy the peaks without returning to the valley from time to time. No one is saying you must start a career or get a real job or that you'll be stuck in your hometown forevermore. Instead, consider returning home as an opportunity to check in, refuel (mentally, physically, and financially), and reassess where life finds you in that moment. Use this time as a guide to where you want to go next.

Natasha

It's an interesting feeling when you know you will soon depart on your next adventure. All the stuck-in-life anxieties slowly dissipate then are quickly replaced with the nerves of counting down. Your stomach will randomly flip-flop for no apparent reason. It's as if your body knows it is both in for an adventure as well as a beating. You innately become more frugal. Last month's shopping spree angers you enough to not even splurge on fast food on a dollar menu. You begin counting costs by what they would be worth on the road, for example that new pair of heels is my four-day hostel budget. That new handbag is a quarter the cost of a flight from Greece to Egypt. Priorities shift to fit in your newfound universe.

    Daydreaming is what gets you into the most trouble at work, though. An entire instructional conversation can be missed while remembering the awe you experienced while first breathing in the salty humidity of Thailand. Or imagining what accent will roll off the lips of your next international lover. Will he love with the passion of the Argentineans? Will he be as protective as the Germans? Or as forward as the Australians? All the while my boss is explaining the importance of the jalapeño's placement in the ten and two positions. It takes every ounce of energy not to walk away or shout "NO ONE REALLY GIVES A SHIT!" Only this job is providing you with the opportunity to finance your next excursion. So I bite my tongue once again, while adjusting the jalapeños to the ten and two positions and resume counting down the days until I leave.

In 2020 COVID-19 upended the world of travel as we knew it. Natasha had to cancel her wedding in Greece twice and between 2019 and 2022 Kim booked, rescheduled, and canceled her trip to Japan three times! Being unable to travel freely or without restriction is frustrating and makes the restlessness that creeps in that much more unbearable, like an itch you can't scratch. Sometimes though, you need to pause and embrace the holding pattern and remember more good times are ahead. Remember, it's a life-time marathon, not a one-time sprint. The idea behind everything we've learned and are trying to express throughout this writing is that, with any luck, you'll continue to nurture your curiosity and zest for learning and that travel will remain a constant throughout your life for years to come.

You might be surprised to find the memories that pull you back into visceral moments of reminiscence aren't the most expected. The very reasons that drew you to explore a specific country, region, city, or town may satisfy an experience, but it's the moments in-between that will tug at you for years to come. Those are moments experienced alone or shared between travelers that can never be recreated. Laughs that can only be experienced once, cheers that can only clink again in your collective memories, meals shared with strangers that became friends, knowing that if you were to reach out to them again today, they would accept your invitation with a ready bottle of wine and a good story. These are the experiences your guidebooks can't prepare you for, and there are a select few words to accurately describe the feeling and memory of it. We know just how special, fleeting, and rare these moments are and wish your journal pages are filled as much with who you met as what you saw and experienced.

Returning home can be difficult for other reasons. You are no longer defined by your county borders and town lines. When you decide to leave the comforts of what you know to explore the world, you become defined by east to west, not simply East Coast to West Coast. Your eyes, bright with wanderlust, can dim if your thirst for adventure remains unquenched for too long. Friends that eagerly inquire about your adventures become bored and possibly resentful of your pursuits. Depending on your social circle, you may be the only one that actively has or wants to travel abroad, let alone in a manner that is less than conventional. That can create a loneliness that, if left malnourished, can eat away at you from the inside.

There are countless stories of people working their entire lives, never taking a vacation, saving their epic adventures for retirement only to die shortly after retiring, never having realized their dreams. What we're proposing is akin to a reverse retirement plan. There is no certainty of tomorrow, so why not live for today? While you will have supporters in your corner, it's worth noting that others may caution you to not lose momentum in either school or career. They may argue that traveling for an extended period will derail any gains or momentum you've created (school, work, relationships, etc.). While well-meaning, keep in mind that there is nothing lost in exploring countries and cultures outside of what you know. You only have knowledge, empathy, and understanding to gain.

Kim - Reflections on Years Spent Trying to Catch Smoke

My father was my sounding board and lifeline each time I returned home. You see, every subsequent adventure following my first trip abroad was like trying to catch smoke. They were never long enough, and I never wanted them to end. Yet try as I might, I'd find myself back home feeling lost among the all too familiar streets, friends, and patterns I had known growing up.

Whenever we talked about my recent or past travel adventures, his eyes would gleam with tears of pride. He would lift my spirits each time I fell victim to the well-meaning comments from friends or family about my wayward or vagabonding life choices. Even my mother, with all her love and grace, couldn't wrap her head around my continued need to travel and had audible concerns that my fierce independence would ultimately hurt me in future career endeavors or relationships.

We previously spoke about loneliness on the road; however, travel is also a companion. In returning home and not traveling (for however long or short a period that may be) there's a certain loss of identity that can wrap its tentacles around you. A questioning begins to set in when returning to the ordinary, the routine, and the familiar. In many ways I wondered if I'd set my bar too high at such a young age and have simply been trading in longer and longer poles to vault it as the years have moved on. Being back home again felt like wearing clothes that fit better when I was ten pounds lighter. I could get them on, and they still covered my body, but I could no longer move with the same freedom, ease, or comfort as before.

As it happened, my mother had an upcoming trip to Germany planned to visit her family, and I decided to join her over there as a surprise. I was feeling too settled back in Florida and needed to break free of the constraints of normal life. With this trip on the horizon, I also decided it was time to break up with my high school sweetheart for the last time. It was a callus break that I handled poorly out of fear of both losing him and, more importantly, losing myself. While absolutely nothing was wrong, I just knew it wasn't right for us to remain together even though I loved him deeply. Our relationship had rekindled many times over the years despite my travel escapades and his time overseas in the military. When we were apart, →

we lived freely but, like magnetic poles, when we came together it was like coming home.

While vacationing in Germany, I decided to take a few days to travel back to Switzerland and visit my friends the hostel owners who'd once allowed me to use their little slice of heaven as home base during the second half of my yearlong adventure abroad. There is a saying that goes "If heaven ain't what it's cracked up to be, send me back to Gimmelwald." Intuition made me bring my newly obtained German passport along with me. In truth, I was missing my ex and wondering if I'd made the right decision in ending things. I was afraid to go home and fall back into the familiar, convinced that, like satellites, we'd orbit right back into comfortable patterns.

They didn't need an extra set of hands at the hostel but with a German passport now in my possession, my options were less limiting, and they offered to ask around the village to see if anyone else might be keen to hire me on. You see, somewhere between the train ride from Nüremburg to Gimmelwald, I decided to move to Switzerland.

As it happened, just up the mountain, in the neighboring village of Mürren, there was a couple who ran a guest house, bar, and restaurant who needed a bartender. After an informal interview where I demonstrated a competent amount of conversational German and a boatload of hospitality experience, I was hired. I had just landed an official job in the Swiss Alps! I was set up with an apartment overlooking the world-famous Eiger, Monk, and Jungfrau Mountains, a Swiss bank account, my training schedule, and list of expected duties. Not having intended to move to Switzerland while on my three-week vacation to Germany, two truths were realized. First, I had to call my boss and let him know I'd quit. Second, I'd just put an ocean between myself and my ex, and I secretly wanted him to cross it to be with me.

Of all my overseas exploits, that was the hardest year abroad for several reasons. I wasn't traveling,

I was working. I'd committed myself to a formal job, paying both taxes and rent. I had a lot of down time to think about the choices that led me here, yet not enough free time to hang out at the Mountain Hostel and commune with like-minded backpackers. I was working in a hotel setting catering to hotel guests. The mindset and guest interactions are different in hotels than in hostels, and I was missing my people!

A few months in, I was embraced as an honorary local, which further established the barrier between myself (a foreigner not travelling) and the throngs of happy backpackers recalling the adventures that had led them to this mountain while prosting pints down in Gimmelwald. Of the very few opportunities I found to make my way down to the Mountain Hostel, what would the odds be that I would know one of the backpackers? We've talked about relationships on the road, and low and behold, there stood a man whom I'd had an intense romantic flirtation with years prior. He was fresh off his most recent adventure, having walked over 500 miles across northern Spain to complete the Camino de Santiago de Compostela. Although our reunion was brief, fate and fortune present themselves in mysterious ways.

Although I hiked almost daily, I was in the worst shape of my life physically, mentally, and emotionally. I drank too much and ate my weight in ice cream. I was twenty-pounds heavier than when I arrived, homesick, lovesick, and sad. After ten out of twelve months, I broke my contractual commitment in Switzerland and returned to Florida feeling no less wayward than before I left. The two years following my return were the beginning of what seemed like a transition into normal life. I was now almost thirty years old, in a good relationship, and at the start of a burgeoning career. I'd discovered rock climbing and quickly fell in with an incredible community of adventure-spirited seekers and climbers. I was once again healthy and, by all outward appearances, life was good.

There's a restlessness that comes when not traveling. You don't even have to be actively on the road, just having your next plane ticket purchased is enough to tamp down the twitchy leg syndrome that comes from not bending the binding on your passport for too long. I was itchy and twitchy and unsettled. As a teacher, I felt like a fraud in my new profession who owed my students and myself more than I was giving, which at the time felt like it should be 110%. →

That summer, I booked a last-minute flight to Florence and spent two weeks bouncing around northern Italy. I drank red wine out of the bottle, ate fresh pasta every day, and sunbathed on the rocks on the shores of the Cinque Terre. It was what I needed in the moment, but still wasn't enough. Upon returning home I dug up what I hoped was still a working email for the man I'd run into back in Switzerland, sent a lengthy apology for how things ended years prior, and peppered him with questions about his experience in Spain. Summer break was coming up and I needed a walkabout.

    Like attracts like and over the years, with very few exceptions, I've worked with and for some of the most fiercely independent, badass, razor-sharp women. My principal and vice principal were no exception to this foundation of support. With their blessing (and the promise to keep a blog for my middle school students to follow), I did not renew my teaching contract for the following school year, and on June 15, I set out with my small JanSport rucksack and blue Nike Frees to walk 500 miles across northern Spain—you guessed it—by myself. This decision set into motion the next ten years of my life's adventures.

    Making the decision to end yet another relationship, give up yet another apartment, and leave yet another job—when all were comfortably sedating but not soulfully satisfying—is scary. But not honoring that call that bellows for you to break out of society's cage will downright extinguish your light. I've learned it's more rewarding to watch the smoke slip between your fingers than to have never captured it at all.

There are a few ways to traverse this existence we call life. You can travel along the paved road, the road less traveled, or climb the mountain in front of you. The paved road is easy. Nearly anyone can walk it, there might be a pothole or two, but it'll get you to where you're trying to go fairly easy. The road less traveled weaves and winds. There are dense patches of fog and sometimes the oasis off in the distance is a mirage. The signposts are less obvious, and the destination is rivaled only in terms of the journey it took you to get there. It's mysterious and alluring and calls to your soul. The mountain offers a challenge to those who dare, usually at a crossroads or a rather comfortable point in their life. It stirs shit up you didn't realize had settled. It will rattle your strength and demand your endurance. You will question if you can even ascend and weep when you reach the pinnacle. Your efforts are never in vain and often are rewarding for years to come.

In trying to catch smoke, the same fire that warms you also warns you of the burns you will endure. Outwardly they're not always obvious. Inwardly you know they're vital to your whole existence.

FUN FACT

Both sunflower images were taken from our separate independent travels along the Camino de Santiago. A fellow Pilgrim advised to stop along the way and dance among the sunflowers.

We hope you find value in our words and experiences and if you're still nervous to travel alone, simply take us with you. The world is both imperfect and achingly beautiful and not to be missed. So, open your laptop, smart phone, or tablet, pour a glass of something bubbly, pick a bucket list item, and book your flight. You can figure the rest out when you arrive. Embrace the unknown. You've got this!

Be audacious. Become irreverent. Travel, even if you must dance in the sunflowers alone.

PRO-TIP
★ ★ ★ ★ ★ ★ ★

It's easy to believe you could never forget the details of an epic adventure, however you can and you may. Therefore, when you find yourself in a memorable location or situation, do the following:

1. Swing into a tourist shop and pick up a postcard.
2. Fill it out with a highlight of your experience, who you met, where you were, or any other memorable content (including the date).
3. Mail it to yourself back home. You will love looking back on all the stamps and colors.
4. Once home, bind all of your postcards (in chronological order) into a one-of-a-kind, handmade journal from your recent trip.

This is an inexpensive and unique-to-you travel memento that will be treasured for the rest of your life!

11 More Bucket List Ideas
To check off your list

91. Free dive in Mato Grosso, Brazil ☐
92. Zip line at sunset in Trentinara, Italy ☐
93. Ride a "seahorse" in the Leeward Antilles Island of Bonaire, Caribbean Netherlands ☐
94. Visit the Big Cat Sanctuary in Kent, United Kingdom ☐
95. Traverse the Quezaltepeque Volcano inside El Boqueron National Park, El Salvador, then tube down the rainbow slide in El Boqueron ☐
96. Run across a squishy bog in Kathmandu, Nepal ☐
97. Sleep in the pointed-hat village of Alberobello, Italy ☐
98. Discover your next novel at the infinity book tower in Prague, Czech Republic ☐
99. Bungee jump at SkyPark, Russia's longest suspended pedestrian bridge ☐
100. Catch a train ride through Maeklong Railway Market in Bangkok, Thailand ☐
101. Backpack all or part of the historic Silk Road trade route including Turkey, Greece, Iran, Kazakhstan, Uzbekistan, Tajikistan, Kyrgyzstan, and China ☐

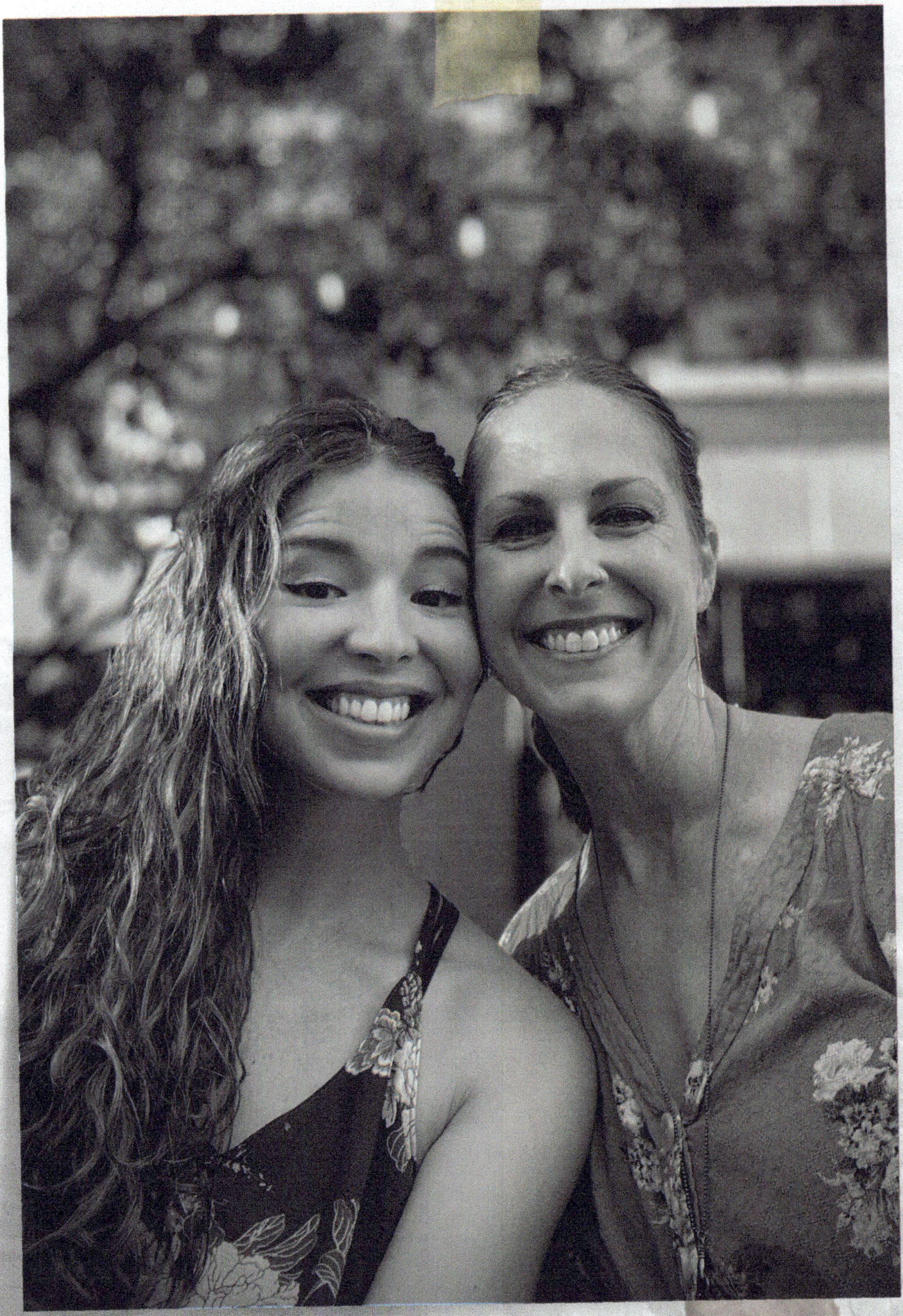

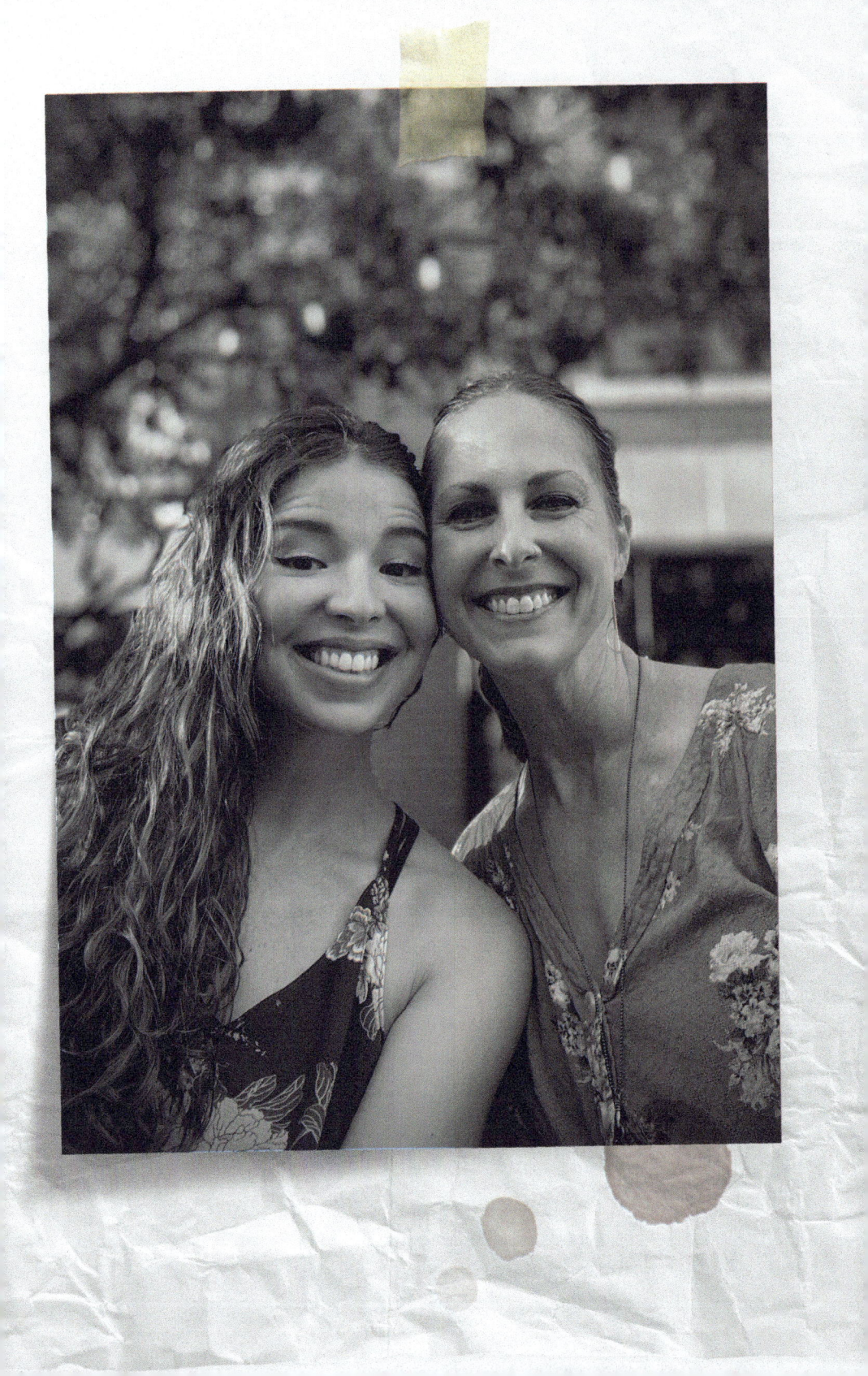

Acknowledgements

To everyone who ever told us we were brave or that they wish they could travel alone like we did, thank you for your raw honesty and sharing your fears and concerns. We wrote this for you. To that point, this book would not have been possible without the unending support and persistence of our families and friends reminding us we have a story worth sharing and encouraging us to finish. To Joe, Phil, Pyper, and Marcel, it's fair to say we couldn't have crossed the finish line without your limitless love and encouragement. Thank you and we love you!

To our editor Kelsey, thank you for your keen eye, creative guidance, and thoroughly believing that our stories will resonate with other women who dream of traveling. To Simon our creative designer, just "wow!" Your spirit of adventure in bringing our book to life was everything we could have hoped for and more.

Natasha would like to give special thanks and photo credits to Alex Rushing for his stunning image of hot air balloons in Turkey, Nicholas Eley for capturing the spirit of Nepal, Jessica Lumm for making me a mermaid for a day, and Lindsey Samuels for taking photos of our time in Asia and the permissions to share them with the world. Kim would like to thank Luca Trovato & Everett Kennedy Brown for their inspiring journal images of Mongolia that led her to explore the country, and their expressed permissions to feature them.

Thank you to all the travelers, hosts, hostel owners, transit drivers, pilots, conductors, road angels, strangers, friends, and incredible humans we have met around the world who took us in or got us safely from point A to point B each and every time. You epitomize all that is good in the world and give us strength to venture out again and again knowing our paths are likely to cross.

To all the women reading this and those who dare to dream bigger than your hometown borders and life's constraints: thank you for bringing our story into your hearts. Our greatest wish is that in reading this book you're emboldened to travel, anywhere and everywhere, even if it means going it alone.

While the technologies may change the heart and soul of the backpacking community remains tangible, timeless, and approachable. We hope you find everything you never realized you were looking for.

Peace, Love & Coddiwomples

Kim & Natasha

Country Ideas for Backpacking on a Budget

From $20 Day
- Bolivia
- Cambodia
- Laos
- Nepal
- Ethiopia
- Malawi
- Ghana
- Nicaragua
- India
- Vietnam

From $35 Day
- Thailand
- Guatemala
- Mongolia
- Ecuador
- Malaysia
- Myanmar
- Sri Lanka
- Peru
- Indonesia
- Egypt
- Paraguay
- Iran
- Morocco
- Kenya
- Uzbekistan

Memories & Makeshift Souvenirs

Tuck these mementos in your travel journal with a little note for you to look back on years later when you need a reminder of the badass traveler you are!

- Newspaper clippings from the local travel or culture section of country you're traveling through
- Train, flight, or bus ticket stubs
- Concert or foreign movie tickets
- Hostel check – in cards
- Random city flyers
- Beverage coasters or unique sugar packets
- Country patches (sew them onto your backpack)
- Postcards – not just for mailing
- Business cards from hostels, restaurants, and hotels you really enjoyed
- Museum entry ticket stubs
- Matchbooks from cool bars or nightclubs
- Pressed flowers or leaves
- Small stones – write the location and date with a felt-tip pen (don't collect too many or they will weigh your pack down!)
- Contacts journal – Bring a small (separate) journal in which you only collect written notes and contact info from travelers you meet along the way. Reading these years later (versus inputting their number in your phone or exchanging socials) is a uniquely special way to reflect on your travels.

Useful Backpacker Websites Just a few to get you started

The resources that follow are simply ideas or suggestions to help get the creative and adventurous wheels turning for travel ideas. As with anything, this information is current at the time of publication but subject to change.

Passport, Travel & Health Resources

- Obtaining, Renewing, or Replacing a Lost or Stolen US Passport
  www.travel.state.gov
- CDC: Traveler's Health
  www.cdc.gov/travel
- World Health Organization
  www.who.int
- Around the World Tickets
  www.airtreks.com
- Going
  www.going.com
- Travelzoo
  www.travelzoo.com
- ISIC – International Student Identification Card
  www.isic.org
- ISE Visa Debit Card
  www.isecard.com
- ISE Faculty ID Card
  www.isecard.com/faculty-id-card.html
- IYEC – International Youth Exchange Card
  www.isecard.com/youth-id-card.html
- Backpacker Travel Insurance
  www.worldnomads.com
- *Pack Smart and Traveling Light* (article)
  www.ricksteves.com
- Food Allergy Chef Cards
  www.foodallergy.org

Accommodations

- Hostel World
  www.hostelworld.com
- Hostelz
  www.hostelz.com
- Hosteling International
  www.hihostels.com
- Hostels Club
  www.hostelsclub.com
- HI USA
  www.hiusa.org
- Couch Surfing
  www.couchsurfing.com
- WWOOF International
  www.wwoofinternational.org
- WWOOF USA
  www.wwoofusa.org

Backpacker Adventure Busses

- TruTravels
  www.trutravels.com
- The Dragon Trip
  www.thedragontrip.com
- The Green Toad Bus
  www.greentoadbus.com
- Kiwi Experience
  www.kiwiexperience.com
- MacBackpackers
  www.macbackpackers.com
- Stray Travel
  www.straytravel.com

Backpacker Cars

- Backpacker Cars – Australia
  www.backpacker-cars.com
- Backpacker Cars – New Zealand
  www.backpackercar.co.nz
- AAA – International Drivers Permit
  www.aaa.com

Crewing Around the World

- Crew Seekers
  www.crewseekers.net
- Find a Crew
  www.findacrew.net

Dog Sled Tours

- The Mushing Coop – Alaska
  www.themushingcoop.com
- Expedition Greenland
  www.expeditiongreenland.com

International Motor Bike Tours

- Ride Expeditions
  www.rideexpeditions.com
- Two Wheeled Expeditions
  www.twowheeledexpeditions.com
- Eidleweiss Bike Travel
  www.edelweissbike.com
- Motourismo
  www.motourismo.com

Trains

The options to travel by train globally, are plentiful.

- Australia
  www.australiatrains.com
- European Rail Travel
  www.eurail.com
  www.interrail.eu
  www.raileurope.com
- India
  www.deccan-odyssey-india.com
- Japan
  www.global.jr-central.co.jp
- South America
  www.railsouthamerica.com
- Trans-Siberian | Trans-Mongolian
  www.transiberianexpress.net
  www.intrepidtravel.com →

Teach, Study, Volunteer Abroad

- Gap Year
  www.gapyearassociation.org
- Go Abroad
  www.goabroad.com
- Peace Corps
  www.peacecorps.gov
- Study Abroad
  www.studyabroad.state.gov
- Teach English Abroad
  www.ciee.org
- Volunteer Abroad
  www.gooverseas.com
- WWOOF
  www.wwoofinternational.org

Interesting Reads

- Solo Female Traveler – Blog
  news.airtreks.com
- As We Travel | Travel the World
  aswetravel.com
- *How To Travel Confidently on Your Period*
  worldnomads.com
- *It's Time to End the Stigma: The Global Issues Surrounding Menstruation*
  thegoodtrade.com
- Global Oral Contraception Availability
  archive.ocsotc.org
- *Safe Travels: Birth Control When You're Abroad*
  bedsider.org
- *Puerto Rico Debates Who Put Out the Lights in Mosquito Bay*
  nytimes.com
- *A Lament for Afghanistan What Am I Doing Here* –
  by Bruce Chatwin
- *Around the World by Sailboat*
  transitionsabroad.com
- *10 Modern Travel Words*
  huffpost.com
- *How to Cross the Ocean on a Freighter Ship*
  artofmanliness.com
- *International Backpacking 101*
  artofmanliness.com
- *London man tells of 'shock' jailing in Dubai over kiss*
  bbc.com
- Laird Hamilton, Gabrielle Reece, Brian Mackenzie –
  Interview with Tim Ferriss, Episode 89
  tim.blog/podcast

Inspiring Media

* *Anthony Bourdain's Parts Unknown*
* *Anthony Bourdain's No Reservations*
* *Samantha Brown*
* *Rick Steves*
* *Globe Trekker (YouTube/streaming)*
* *TasteMade Travel (streaming)*
* *180 Degrees South (documentary)*
* *The Secret Life of Walter Mitty (movie)*
* *Eat, Pray, Love (movie/book)*
* *Into the Wild (movie/book)*
* *The Way (movie)*
* *Vagabonding (book)*

Songs To Inspire

- "The Road I Must Travel" – The Nightwatchman
- "Taro" – alt-J
- "Reckoning Song" – Asaf Avidan
- "Waka Waka (This Time for Africa)" – Shakira
- "Fast Car" – Tracy Chapman
- Into the Wild soundtrack – Eddie Vedder
- "On the Road Again" – Willie Nelson
- "Vacation" – Dirty Heads
- "Road to Nowhere" – Talking Heads
- "Here I Go Again" – Whitesnake
- "Free Fallin'" – Tom Petty
- "Down Under" – Men at Work

These lists could go on, and on, and on. Or you could write the next new blog or book about it, after your next epic adventure, adding insight and value to the future aspiring solo female traveler. We hope you find the inspiration to set forth and explore. Safe and happy travels!

My Bucket List

No.
Date

My Packing List

No.
Date

My Budget

No. _____
Date

My First Solo Travel Journal Entry

No.
Date

Index

A
Accommodations   37, 139-173
Affection   185, 189
Airbnb (Vrbo)   165
Allergies   103, 217

B
Backpacker   24, 117
Backpacking   24, 29, 117, 252
Birth Control   133-135
Bratpackers   116, 121
Boats   78-79, 81
Borders & Crossings   52-55
Bucket List Ideas   42, 61, 93, 114, 136, 175, 198, 220, 232, 248
Busses   73-77, 254

C
Camping   167-168
Cars (Personal Vehicles)   69-71, 255
Common Rooms   153-158
Condoms   133, 134, 208
Couch Surfing   139, 161-163, 170
Cultural Courtesies   183-184

D
Discounts   33, 144
Documents (Documentation)   46, 49, 212
Drinking   25, 197, 218

E
Eating   216
Electronics   121-124

F
Feminine Hygiene   128-132
Flashpackers   117
Food Allergy   212, 216-218, 254
Fun Facts (Did You Know)   40, 47, 50, 60, 75, 196, 247

G
Gap Year   87, 256

H
Hitchhiking   72
Homestays   166, 170
Hostels   140-160
Hostel Etiquette   148
Hotels   169, 171

I
Illness   103
Immunizations   58

K
Kim's Stories   10, 23, 45, 56, 67, 70, 76, 79, 83, 85, 97, 102, 105, 113, 122, 133, 149, 151, 181, 202, 210, 217, 219, 227, 238, 243

L
Lock Outs   147
Love on the Road   203-209

M
Menstruation (Periods)   128-132
Money   32, 213-215

N
Natasha's Stories   14, 39, 50, 54, 77, 83, 84, 88, 101, 118, 124, 128, 130, 143, 155, 158, 160,163, 179, 193, 195, 203, 205, 235, 240

P
Packing   119-127
Passport   44-50
Pro Tips   36, 37, 48, 51, 56, 68-71, 73, 79, 91, 96, 99, 103, 129, 133, 141, 145, 148, 153-156, 158, 187, 190, 193, 197, 214, 248

R
Religion (Politics)   180

S
Safety   72, 77, 144, 172, 189, 212
Scams   110-112
Sex (also see Birth Control)   207-208
Solitude (Loneliness)   223-231
Stuck (Breakdowns, Delays, Disasters, etc.)   95-105
Study Abroad   87, 256

T
Tipping   194
Toilets   156, 191
Train   64-67, 255
Transportation   36, 63-83
Travel Insurance   103-104, 254

U
Unsolicited Attention   187

V
Vaccines   58-59
Valuables (bling)   212
Visas   48-50
Volunteer   91, 148, 256

W
Walking (Hiking, Trekking)   85
Water   59, 154-155, 191, 218-219
WWOOFing   167, 170, 254

263

Made in the USA
Columbia, SC
28 October 2023